REVIEWS

"Every time I meet a business start-up or CEO, I will give them this book and say, 'just start here'".

Michael Bowyer, Former CTO Siemens Enterprise Communications

"Too often advice like this is wrapped up in a lot of mumbo jumbo that is more about the ego of the author than about trying to communicate with a novice audience. Ian's short stories explain important business issues very simply".

Craig Wilson, Former VP EMEA, HP Enterprise

"I like the structure of the book with the simple messages at the end of the anecdotes. It is amazing how many businesses have gone bust because they haven't really considered these basic fundamentals".

Alex Larcombe, Sales Director

"I particularly liked the 'Six Weeks to Launch' story in the Product Development chapter as this is something that is massively overlooked".

Gary Noble, Head of IT

"Probably my favourite section is People, especially 'the same people can be good, bad and average'. I see that a lot, even in myself and it's something for me to work on".

Stevie Ridsdale, IT Support

"I like the 'HATS' story and the suggested approach to how you recruit staff"

Manuel Cristelo, Software Development Manager

DEDICATION

I dedicate this book to

Julie, Carmen and Claudia

I achieved a lot in my career,

but,

I also spent too much time at work

CONTENTS

Introduction	9
Who is This For?	10
Why Listen to Me?	15
Chapter One	21
You Go Bust, When You Run Out of Cash	22
Amazon, Netflix, Tesla and WeWork	24
I'm Making Profit, But My Cash Isn't Going Up	28
Entrepreneurs Who Didn't Have Much Schooling	30
Which Is Your Worst Month, For Cash?	32
Graph Your Daily Cash Balance	34
A Strong Debt Collector Is Priceless	36
You'd Never Walk Out of a Restaurant Without Paying	38
Why More Sales Can Actually Kill Your Business	40
Why Spreadsheets are like Wine	42
The Perfect Cash Forecast - Regular and Often	44
Learn from The Market Stall	46
Crowd Funding - How Not to Give Away Equity	48
Chapter Two	51
The Economics of One	52
Which Makes More Money - Cafes or Restaurants?	54
Beware of Using the Wrong Number	56
How to use Page 3 Pricing	58
How to encourage people to buy more products	60
A Disaster Waiting to Happen	62
There Is No Such Thing as A Sexy Pound	64

The Problem with Enterprise Customers	66
Where Should the Managing Director Sit?	68
Good News Travels Fast	70
Salespeople have to cover their own costs	72
Beware of Creating an Accidental Frankenstein	74
Consider Success-Only Selling	76
Who Should Select Suppliers?	78
How Do You Get Economies of Scale in Support Costs?	80
Chapter Three	85
The Most Important Thing - Respect	86
HATS - Hire Attitude, Train Skill	88
How to Set Targets	90
What can we learn from Alex Ferguson?	92
I Like Me, Let's Get Another One	94
Getting It Wrong When Hiring	96
The Problem of Short Attention Spans	98
No Negs On My Team	100
Delegation Depends	102
Too Many People Wanting Promotion at Once	104
Now You Are Through the Door	106
Remembering Names in Large Organisations	108
Employees and Shareholders Are Sometimes Different	110
Why the Bosses Face Is Important	112
The Same People Can Be Good, Bad and Average	114
You Can't Shout at Plants	116
If You are The Most Junior in The Room	118
Why Shadowing Is So Powerful	120

Doing Presentations - Home and Away ... 122

Successful People Fail ... 125

Chapter Four ... 129

The Potters' Wheel ... 130

If It Looks Too Good to Be True ... 131

The Cat and The Bell ... 132

Churn and The Switching Process ... 134

Common Sense Is Not Common ... 136

What You Measure Is What You Get ... 138

What Should You Measure? ... 140

What Should You Worry About? ... 142

There Are At Least 2 Ways to Achieve the Same Result ... 144

Faces Not Numbers ... 146

The 2 x 2-Seater Sofa Meeting Rule ... 148

Stick to What You Are Good At ... 150

The How-to-End-a-Meeting Rule ... 152

Give the Woman A Chicken ... 154

Facts versus Emotions: Staffing Models ... 157

Chapter Five ... 161

Six Weeks from Launch ... 162

How to Choose A Supplier? ... 164

Leading Edge or Bleeding Edge? ... 166

Innovation Is 169

Chapter Six ... 173

What is Capital Expenditure? ... 174

The Only Thing I've Learned About Pubs and Restaurants ... 176

Not All Capital Expenditure Is Equal ... 178

The Difference Between Simple and Complex Capex	180
Evaluating Complex Capex - Functionality or Volume?	182
Chapter Seven	185
How to Make Maths Your Friend	186
Why the Tin-of-Beans Rule saves time	188
How Do You Spot A Spreadsheet You Should Not Trust?	190
When 'Nearly' Is Good Enough	192
The Law Of 78	194
That's Not What I Expected	196
Beware of Spurious Accuracy	199
Chapter Eight	203
An Easy Way to Find Operational Process Problems	204
Play Chess Not Draughts	206
The One-Side-of-A4 Business Plan	208
The Top-3-Things Rule	211
Chapter Nine	215
Banks sell money	216
Should I borrow from a bank?	218
How Does Bank Lending Work? The Basics	220
When you need more than one bank	222
What is Asset-backed lending?	224
Borrowing against Intellectual Property	226
What is Cashflow lending?	228
Why interest rates are never as low as you expect	231
Bank Covenants - the rules you must obey	234
Revolving Credit Facilities and Accordions	237
What is a Convertible Loan?	240

Is this the real reason, why Thomas Cook failed? 243

Chapter Ten 247

Why We Really Floated On AIM 248

Running Public and Private Companies 250

Chapter Eleven 253

Why nothing should be decided by One-Man-One-Vote 254

Inside and outside of the meeting 256

Shareholders - Agree or Argue? 258

How to Use A Chairman or Boss? 260

Chapter Twelve 265

The Personalised Hat Trick 266

Something Only for You 268

Recessions - What Typically Happens 270

Business Is A Problem-Solving Exercise 272

Chapter Thirteen 275

Planning the handover 276

If It Was Easy, Everyone Would Be Doing It 279

INTRODUCTION

Introduction

Tips from a
3 x Winner
UK CEO of the Year

THE STREET SMART MBA

Mastering Business Acumen

WHO IS THIS FOR?

When you start a new business, or work in one, no-one tells you how hard it will be and how often you will probably fail at something. There does not seem to be anywhere to go to learn practical tips and advice. Everyone would love to have a kindly mentor figure who had been there before and got the T-shirt. Someone who could dish out sage advice and a few calming words when it seemed to be going wrong.

I can't mentor all of you, but I was the boss for almost 30 years, so I will try to help with over 100 short anecdotes and practical tips. Some will be applicable to where you are today in your career; other stories and tips you might come back to later (such as how to borrow money from banks).

For many people maths and numbers are terrifying, and in this book, you can learn how to demystify and simplify these things. The people who helped me proofread this text often described parts of this book as 'simplified business maths for business owners.' You will learn that you do not need to be good at maths to be successful at business. We'll look at some simple maths tricks that might make things less daunting.

People remember stories: things that they can repeat and tell their friends. Straightforward lessons are boring. Stories, particularly ones that people can relate to, are interesting.

I have found myself repeating the same stories over and over again to the thousands of people who have worked for me, so I have finally decided to write them down. These are the things that I picked up over the years that proved incredibly useful to me.

A failure early on in your career can often be a great way to learn. Let me tell you a true story about something that happened to me.

I started my senior management career at GEC-Marconi. I only had one face-to-face budget meeting with the great Lord Weinstock, but it left a lasting impression. Lord Weinstock had started with relatively little and built a cash pile of around £2 billion (in the 1980's). He was being criticised for not knowing where to invest the £2 billion?[1] I simply wanted to meet the man who had amassed £2 billion in cash from next to nothing. It was an astonishing achievement. I now had a new ambition (that I never even got close to achieving) - to amass £2 billion in cash and get accused of not knowing what to do with it.

Knowing of his reputation for detail, I revised my numbers, for nearly a week. I fell over at his very first question. He was the master of commanding a room by speaking very quietly. He simply asked, "Was your bank balance at the end of the last financial year bigger than the year before? And if not, where did the money go?"

I struggled for what seemed to be the longest hour of my life so far. It took me weeks to realise that I had been given an absolute master class, in business management, in just one meeting. I want to explore and share with you many of the lessons that he started.

Technology changes constantly, but the idea 'cash is king' will never change. You will learn some ideas on things to consider when developing new products and spending money on capital expenditure. If you don't know what

---

[1] Feder, B.J. 1984. NEW YORK TIMES, *The Master Builder of Britain's Electrical Empire*. [online]. Available at <https://www.nytimes.com/1984/09/02/business/the-mater-builder-of-britain-s-electricla-empire.html> [Accessed on 9 February 2020]

capital expenditure is then don't worry; there is a specific chapter on this later on.

The operational advice in the book applies regardless of what sector you work in. No matter how good you are at what you do, you will never succeed without a great team around you. The days of people working for one firm all their life, are now long gone. Finding great people is only part of the problem. You also need to excite them into staying.

One of the things that I knew nothing about when I set up my own business was business lending. Like many I was wary of banks. I wrote the section on business bank borrowing because these are the types of things that would have made my life much easier if someone had taken the time to explain them to me early on.

When I was CEO of AdEPT for 16 years, my Chairman and long-time mentor was Roger Wilson. He often used to say, "The best businesses are created by people who love what they do and find a way of making money doing it."

As I was writing this book, I shared parts of it with experienced businesspeople and complete novices. Interestingly, they all asked the same question, "Who is the book aimed at? Who should read it?" After pondering that for a while my answer is that several different types of people might benefit from reading this …

New Start-ups

In 2001 the UK had 3.3 million self-employed people. By 2017 this had grown to 4.8 million. Almost 15% of the entire UK workforce is self-employed[2].

In hindsight, when I set up my own business, I had some huge advantages: I was 42 years old and had already managed businesses with sales of up to £250 million a year. I was lucky enough to have been allowed to study for an MBA - a 'Masters' Degree in Business Administration'.

Most self-employed startup businesses are run by people who are young, inexperienced, or both. I do not think you have to go to Business School to learn. There are some things you can only learn on the streets by talking and listening to people. That is why I called this book *'The Street-Smart MBA – Mastering Business Acumen - without going to school'.*

---

[2] OFFICE OF NATIONAL STATISTICS, 2018. *Trends in self-employment in the UK.* [online]. Available at
<https://www.ons.gov.uk/employmentandlabourmarket/peopleinwork/employmentandemployeetypes/articles/trendsinselfemploymentintheuk/2018-02-07> [Accessed on 9 February 2020]

Many new startup businesses fail quite quickly. ECI Partners, one of the UK's leading private equity companies shared a staggering fact in their ECI Growth Index 2019, "It is sobering to note that only 40% of [UK] businesses formed in 2012 are still trading five years on. This fact surely underscores that we should celebrate the winners within this 40% and champion the cause of growth businesses going forward". [3]

If you are starting a business, or just considering it, then I hope that my tips and advice will help a few more new businesses to survive and prosper.

Small Businesses That Want to Grow

Let's be honest with ourselves; growing a business is stressful and difficult. I know because I started a business in my spare bedroom and 15 years later it was valued at £100 million (although given the vagaries of the Stock Market, some days it is around £80 million). I have lived through a lot of the business growing pains and I hope I have some lessons to share that might speed your journey.

Managers

If you are on the first rungs of management and want to know more; then this is aimed at you. You should always read a lot. Be keen to understand how other people have become successful. There isn't only one way and there have been many people who have been much more successful than me.

Students

If you are thinking of starting a career in business; then this might help.

Each of the ideas or stories are quite short. This is not a textbook. It is designed for you to be able to dip into it and read a few stories whenever you have the time. I have added a doodle to each story. Partly because doodling was fun, but mainly because I believe that people remember images easier than words.

I hope you find everything interesting and thought-provoking, but if only three or four stories strike a chord and you use them regularly, then this book will have been worthwhile. We all start from a different place, with different knowledge and background, so it is almost certain that it won't be the same stories that strike a chord with each reader. I worked with a huge number of proofreaders. When I asked them, which was their favourite story, they all picked a different one.

---

[3] Sean Whelan, 2019. *ECI Growth Index 2019 Executive Summary*. [PDF] Available online at <https://www.ecipartners.com/~/media/Files/E/ECI-Partners/The%20ECI%20Growth%20Index%202019.pdf> Accessed on 25 Feb 2020

I hope you find the book useful and that I make you smile along the way because that is the first tip:

Be serious, but not too serious, because if you are then no-one will want to work with you.

WHY LISTEN TO ME?

When you set yourself up as someone offering advice and tips then the obvious question from any reader is 'Why should I listen to you?"

In this section I try to give a few reasons why I might be worth spending a few minutes with.

I achieved what is probably the 'Ultimate Dream' of a New Business Owner - From A Spare Bedroom to £100 million

In 2003 I started AdEPT in a spare bedroom. In October 2018 it was valued on the London Stock Exchange Alternative Investment Market (AIM) at £101 million.[4] At the time of publishing in early 2020, the value of our business like

---

[4] London Stock Exchange, 2018. *Adept Technology Group share price 3rd October*

many others, has almost halved with the rise of the Coronavirus threat. We now face the challenge of rebuilding it.

29 Consecutive Years of Rising Profitability (EBITDA)

I started as a Managing Director/Chief Executive in 1990 and finally stood down as a CEO and became part-time Chairman at the end of 2018.

If you are not an accountant and do not understand what EBITDA (Earnings Before Interest Tax and Depreciation) means, don't worry; it is simply the operating profit measure that gives you the best estimate of a business's cashflow. In the rest of the book (except for the section on bank borrowing), I'll simply refer to profit; when I technically mean EBITDA.

For 29 consecutive years, despite several financial crises and massive changes in technology, I reported increased profit every year.

Some of the sections in the book will look at how you can keep yourself motivated over such a long period and how you can train yourself to never give in.

One of only Three Companies on AIM to grow Earnings per Share for 10 Consecutive Years

It is quite astonishing how hard it is to achieve consistent growth, so don't beat yourself up if you cannot achieve it every year. To put this into some context, consider this …

There are almost 1,000 companies on AIM (the Alternative Investment Market), the part of the London Stock Exchange dedicated to smaller companies. Only three companies (AdEPT - my company, iomart and Churchill China) managed to grow Earnings Per Share for 10 consecutive years (2008 to 2018).[5]

We must have done something right.

Along the Way I Won A Few Awards

If you are the type of person who is impressed by badges, then this bit is probably for you. Along the way I won a few awards. No-one ever tells you why you have been awarded something, so I can only guess. I suspect it was because of the unusually long, 29-year run, of rising profitability.

2018. [online]. Available at <https://www.londonstockexchange.com/exchange/prices-and-markets/stocks/summary/company-summary-chart.html?fourWayKey=GB00B0WY3Y47GBGBXASX1> [Accessed on 31 January 2020]

[5] Factset Analysis, 2019. [online]. Available at <https://www.adept-technology-group.co.uk> [Accessed on 9 February 2020]

In 2016, at the European CEO of the Year Awards, Corporate Vision (CV) magazine named me as UK CEO of the Year. Later in 2016, Technology, Media and Telecom (TMT) magazine also named me as UK CEO of the Year.

In 2017, Acquisitions International magazine named me as their London CEO of the Year. Later in 2017, at the ACQ5 Global Awards, I had the honour of being named as UK Game-changer of the Year for my work on converging the Telecoms and IT sectors.

In 2018, my final year as a CEO, at the Global 100 Awards, I was named for a 3rd time as UK CEO of the Year.[6]

---

[6] See 'About the Author' for awards logos

UK - GAMECHANGER OF THE YEAR
IAN FISHWICK, ADEPT TELECOM PLC

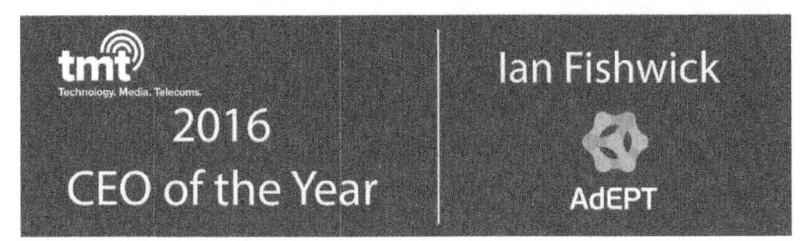

ACQ5 Global Awards 2017

AI 2017 CEO of the Year

Ian Fishwick
AdEPT Telecom PLC
Ceo of the Year - London

tmt 2016 CEO of the Year | Ian Fishwick — AdEPT

CV MAGAZINE

2016 EUROPEAN CEO of the Year Awards
Ian Fishwick
AdEPT Telecom plc
UK

CHAPTER ONE
Cash Is King

YOU GO BUST, WHEN YOU RUN OUT OF CASH

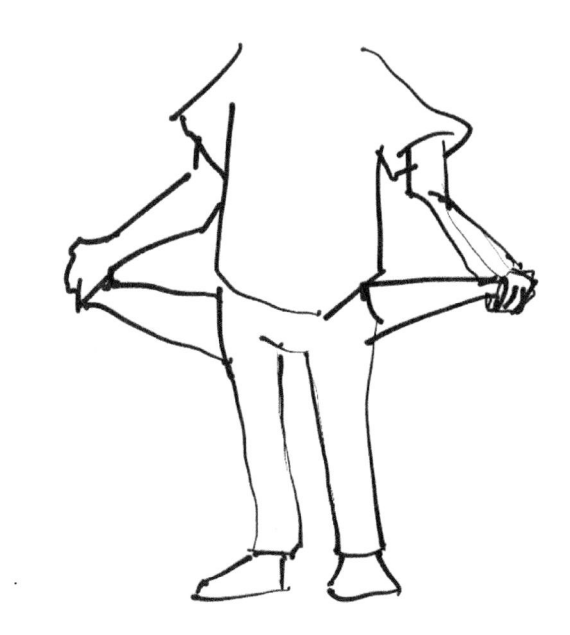

If you have £10 in your pocket and then you spend it all; you have no cash left. If you then receive a bill to pay but you have no money then you go bust, bankrupt, into administration - whatever phrase you want to use.

You must never forget the very simple statement:

YOU GO BUST WHEN YOU RUN OUT OF CASH

You can run a loss-making business for years if you have enough cash to spend. Let's do an example …

If you have £100 million and you lose £20 million in cash every year, then you can survive for 5 years before you go bust. That is a very important point: you can survive short-term losses if you have enough cash to pay your bills.

MY MESSAGE IS SIMPLE

Losing money and going bust is not necessarily the same. If you lose money, then you are spending more cash than you are bringing in and we all know from our daily lives that you cannot spend more than you earn for an indefinite period. Eventually you will run out of money.

AMAZON, NETFLIX, TESLA AND WEWORK

Recent times have seen a new phenomenon: people setting up companies that lose huge amounts of money for several years. Companies such as Amazon, Netflix and Tesla. Does this mean a company does not need to make money anymore? The simple answer is no; although I understand why young entrepreneurs in start-up companies may disagree. Let's take a look at each of these examples to see what we can learn.

Amazon

Amazon was founded in July 1994 and first made a profit in the last quarter of 2001.[7] Over those seven years it spent billions of pounds. How did it survive

---

[7] Alison Griswold & Jason Karaian 1 Feb 2018. *It took Amazon 14 years to make as much in net profit as it did last quarter.* [online]. Available at

for seven years without making a profit? Answer - it persuaded shareholders and banks to invest billions of dollars in the hope that one day it would be big enough to make lots of money - and it worked.

Netflix

Netflix is a TV phenomenon. Its streaming service now supplies over 130 million customers in over 190 countries. For the first few years Netflix showed programmes made by other companies. As Netflix has become more successful there is now a danger that some of those companies will set up their own streaming TV service and stop allowing Netflix to show their content. We can already see giants like Disney looking seriously at competing with Netflix.

Netflix knows that it has to produce more of its own TV content if it is not to be potentially held to ransom by the major TV content providers. It is therefore spending billions of dollars, producing new TV shows, using borrowed money. Netflix's long-term debt stood at $10.4bn at the end of December 2018[8] up from $6.5bn at the end of 2017.

Netflix is making just over $500 million profit a year. Put another way - if profit does not improve then it will take nearly 20 years to pay off the $10.4 billion of debt. I very much doubt that banks will wait that long, so, profits better improve soon.

Tesla

Elon Musk put virtually all the money he made from selling PayPal to eBay into creating Tesla. In 2008 Tesla was tiny and it nearly ran out of money. It was saved by a huge fundraising: the first of several. It took another four years before we saw a production version of the Model S in 2012.

In April 2018, Jim Collins at Forbes did a review of the financial history of Tesla. Tesla makes massive losses and Elon Musk is brilliant at persuading shareholders and banks to invest billions of dollars in his idea. Since the year of its IPO (flotation on the Stock Exchange) in 2010, Tesla has raised $19 billion in capital and produced negative cash flow of $9 billion.

In the past three years, Tesla has lost $3 billion on an operating basis and spent $6.3 billion on capital. That is not a sustainable operating business model. It is entirely dependent upon Elon Musk being able to raise more cash

---

<https://qz.com/1196256/it-took-amazon-amzn-14-years-to-make-as-much-net-profit-as-it-did-in-the-fourth-quarter-of-2017/> [Accessed on 27 Feb 2020]

[8] Variety, 2019. *Netflix to Raise Another $2 Billion Through Debt to Fund Massive Content Spending*. [online]. Available at:
<https://variety.com/2019/digital/news/netflix-debt-junk-bond-2-billion-content-spending-1203377007/> [Accessed on 21 October 2019]

when he needs it in the hope that one day they will produce and sell enough cars to justify the share price.

The longer it takes Tesla to make a profit, the more time the existing major car manufacturers have to catch up and mass produce electric cars.

At the end of 2018, Tesla was trading at a mere 13,690 times its trailing profit, or last years' profit.[9]

In September 2019, only weeks after Tesla had raised another $2.7 Billion, Elon Musk announced that they only had 10 months cash left.[10] In the first 6 months of the year they reported $10.9 Billion of sales but lost $1 Billion.

How big does Tesla need to get before it starts to make money?

Tesla has almost single-handedly persuaded the world that electric cars are viable and desirable. That does not necessarily mean that he will be the great beneficiary of electric cars as the other manufacturers try to catch up. Let's wait and see.

Restaurants

Let's remember that for every big success there are thousands of business failures. A study by Restaurant Brokers concluded that 90% of independent restaurants close within the first year. Why is that? Because they do not have enough cash to pay their bills. The Restaurant Brokers study recommends that to have enough money to operate properly, fledgling restaurants should have enough money in the bank to cover their immediate costs plus an additional food and beverage reorder, two payroll cycles and six months of rent.[11]

WeWork

Still don't believe me. Well, let's look at WeWork.

In the summer of 2019, WeWork planned to float on the New York Stock exchange in September with a valuation of $47 billion. The company hired out office space in over 500 locations in 111 cities around the world. The planned flotation was met with a hostile response from potential investors as

---

[9] Jim Collins, 25 April 2018. *A brief history of Tesla: $19 billion raised and $9 billion of negative cash flow.* [online]. Available at
<https://www.forbes.com/sites/jimcollins/2018/04/25/a-brief-history-of-tesla-19-billion-raised-and-9-billion-of-negative-cash-flow/#10cd119a3d65> Accessed on 27 Feb 2020

[10] Danny Fortson, 2019. Sunday Times 29 September 2019: *Musk races to show Tesla can survive.* Business section

[11] Hannah Wickford, 2018. *The Average Lifespan of a Restaurant.* [online]. Available at: <https://yourbusiness.azcentral.com/average-life-span-restaurant-6024.html> [Accessed on 16 January 2019]

in 2018 WeWork lost $1.9 billion on sales of $1.82 billion. This was double the 2017 loss of $933 million on sales of $886 million.

WeWork was consuming cash at an astonishing rate. Investors were discussing a potential valuation of nearer $10 billion.

This was an incredible drop on the $47 billion target and especially embarrassing for SoftBank who had invested $10 billion in WeWork for a nearly 30% minority stake. The last tranche of investment was $2 billion in January 2019. The stake they were given, for their $2 billion, implied that the whole of WeWork was worth $47 billion.

WeWork decided not to go ahead with the flotation as concerns were also being raised about the behaviour and style of the founder Adam Neumann. He wasn't helped by his decision, to spend $60 million on a private jet, 18 months before the planned flotation.

When the flotation did not go ahead, WeWork ran out of cash very quickly and announced plans for around 2,000 redundancies.

In the end, probably to save at least some of their original investment, Softbank bought WeWork for $8 billion.

No matter how big you are, you go bust, when you run out of cash and it can happen very quickly.

It is easy to get seduced by the one or two giant, famous, businesses that lose money for years. They are in a constant quest to persuade investors and banks to give them more money in the hope that if they get big enough then they will suddenly make loads of money.

However, let's not get negative, let's get savvy - there are thousands of businesses that succeed.

MY MESSAGE IS SIMPLE

Big businesses are no different to small businesses: they go bust when they run out of cash and cannot pay their bills. So, if you plan to lose a lot of money then you need to raise a lot of money first.

I'M MAKING PROFIT, BUT MY CASH ISN'T GOING UP

When you start to make a profit, rather confusingly, it does not necessarily mean that your cash is increasing. Why is that?

There are several potential reasons for cash not rising if you are profitable:

1. You are selling products at a profitable price but some of your customers are not paying their bill
2. The business is profitable, but you are spending cash on capital expenditure (fixed assets such as cars, buildings, machinery etc)
3. You have spent the cash in some other way such as buying another business

4. You have paid a big tax bill. Do not forget that VAT is paid quarterly, and last years' Corporation Tax bill is a long time after the year-end (if you are a small company).

You also need to have a clear understanding of when and how you are going to get paid. I've just had some building repairs done at my house. The builder wanted 50% of his money before he started work, but I would only pay the remaining 50% when I was satisfied that he had completed the work to the quality agreed. Even though the job was profitable for the builder he needed to understand the timing of his cash receipts.

Profits and cash receipts do not always happen at the same time. There are some industries like retail where you get paid immediately the sale is made, but there are many more industries where there is normally some kind of delay before you get paid.

HAVING SAID THAT, the quickest way to spot an accounting fraud is if there is a long spell of profitability but cash does not increase (unless you have spent it on capital expenditure or buying a company).

MY MESSAGE IS SIMPLE

Increasing your profit does not always mean you will also increase your cash.

THERE ARE MANY ENTREPRENEURS WHO DIDN'T HAVE MUCH SCHOOLING

There are a lot of very successful entrepreneurs who never had much schooling. They frequently started in business by selling whatever they could find to make some money.

They often realise the simple truth's that others can forget; you go bust when you run out of cash, not when some complex accounting statement says you have a problem. I am a qualified accountant and I started to think that the more complicated you make things, the more you tend to forget this simple truth.

Many small business owners start to do rudimentary cash flow forecasts probably without even realising it. They worry at night about how they are going to pay their upcoming bills and start to hold cash balances to ensure they are always safe.

I've done about 40 mergers and acquisitions in my life. I kiss a lot of frogs before I find a business I want to buy. That means I have spent many hours looking at the accounts of over five hundred companies and talking to the owners.

I ceased to be surprised at how many businesses of up to £5 million sales per annum still used this simple method of cash forecasting. As one man who ran a business with £5 million sales per annum said, "We always try to keep about £1 million in the bank. We know that even when our tax bills are due, we'll still have about £300,000 cash left and then it builds up again." Their business was extremely financially strong and had been very successful for many years. That simple attitude of ensuring that you never run out of cash is the best way to guarantee survival.

SOMETHING TO WATCH OUT FOR?

It is often interesting to check whether the Managing Director or Chief Executive is a shareholder (or has share options). The reason why I look is that (at the risk of a massive generalisation) people are very happy to spend someone else's money, but, are much more careful with their own. Next time you hear of a company that went bankrupt (ran out of cash) take a look at who was running it: the owner or an employee.

WHICH IS YOUR WORST MONTH, FOR CASH?

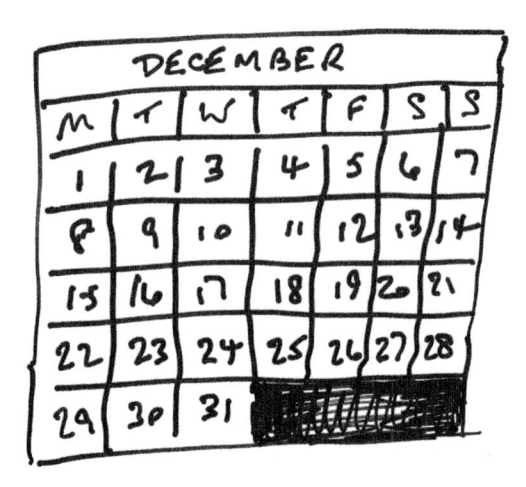

I previously talked about a very successful business owner who knew when his worst month was for cash because he had been running it for several years. If you wait to find out which is your worst month then you might find you cannot pay the bills and you are suddenly in a cash crisis.

It should be relatively easy to guess what your worst month for cash is going to be. Think about:

- Is it when you pay your Corporation Tax each year?

- The guy in the previous story knew that he had a double whammy - once a quarter he had to pay a VAT bill and once a year both the VAT and the Corporation Tax landed in the same month.

- Is your business seasonal? Are there certain months when you have a very big payment to your suppliers?

MY MESSAGE IS SIMPLE

Business is not rocket science. You just need to sit down and think it through.

GRAPH YOUR DAILY CASH BALANCE

When we first started AdEPT, the first thing we did every day was to download last night's closing bank balance and write it down. We then started to graph the closing bank balance to see if there was a pattern. At the end of month two the graph showed a consistent pattern each month. When the graph showed the same pattern again in month three; we knew that was what we should expect and that it would be worse when the quarterly VAT payment was due and the annual Corporation Tax.

Our graph showed cash getting worse in the first half of the month and then increasing rapidly in the last week of the month. Two or three of us sat down to debate why the graph looked like it did. We quickly guessed what was happening.

By the end of week one all our suppliers had invoiced us for services we had bought the previous month. As we were a new business, they insisted on us paying by Direct Debit, the week after their invoice arrived. So, we had a huge outflow of cash in week two. In week three it got worse; because that is when we paid the monthly salary bill. We invoiced our customers in week two but gave them two weeks-notice before we pulled their Direct Debits. That meant that almost all of our cash came in, in week four.

If your business does not show a steady pattern each month then that tells me that you probably have peaks and troughs when you sell things, and you are not selling regular subscription-type services (or recurring revenue as I call it). You then need to plan carefully when you expect sales to peak.

Some businesses are seasonal. I don't just mean the obvious ones like ice cream sales. If you have a business such as an accountant or a lawyer; that sells people's time, then you can probably expect sales to fall in holiday periods such as August and December.

MY MESSAGE IS SIMPLE

Graph your closing cash balance each day - it will become a daily ritual and you will quickly get a very clear understanding of how your business works.

A STRONG DEBT COLLECTOR IS PRICELESS

When people set up businesses they get, understandably, all excited about what they are trying to sell. It is human nature to want to do the things you enjoy and to put off the boring bits. Ringing up people to ask them to pay their bills is about as boring and sometimes stressful, as it gets.

However, it only takes one large customer not to pay you and then you realise that it is financially much better to not have a customer than have one that doesn't pay. Just think about it: you have gone to the expense of buying the product and shipping it to the customer, so, if they don't pay, you are massively out of pocket.

My advice is straightforward: find someone who enjoys collecting money and hire them as one of your very first employees. It is easy to forget how useful they are until one day they are not there and you realise once again the consequences of an unpaid bill. In business it is often the boring bits that make the difference between success and failure.

Humans are like animals in that we can train them to behave in certain ways. Good debt collectors know that if you don't chase a customer immediately as soon as they are late paying a bill then they will assume you are not worried about it. If you let a customer pay a month late, three times in a row, please don't be surprised if they then always pay late.

MY MESSAGE IS SIMPLE

You can train customers to pay on time. Do not forget that customers are sometimes short of cash just like everybody else. If a customer has two bills to pay, but can only afford to pay one of them, who do you think they will pay? The supplier who rings them up or the one that doesn't bother?

Don't forget that everyone who talks to a customer should be a potential debt collector.

YOU WOULD NEVER WALK OUT OF A RESTAURANT WITHOUT PAYING THE BILL

Like the vast bulk of the population I have never walked out of a restaurant without paying the bill. We are either trained to understand that this is the way you behave, or, we do not fancy the idea of an irate owner chasing us down the street. The restaurant has spent money on food and staff to prepare it, so, it seems completely reasonable that we should have to pay the bill.

Why do we think other suppliers do not need to be paid on time? Is it the fact that we cannot see them face-to-face, so, somehow it does not seem as pressing?

In business we have every right to behave like the irate restaurant owner. We cannot necessarily chase customers down the street, but we should not shy from chasing them for the money they owe.

MY MESSAGE IS SIMPLE

If they refuse to pay, then we owe it to the rest of the business community to help flag up, who are the villains who will take your goods and services and never pay for them? That is why I am happy to serve County Court Judgement Notices on customers who do not pay. The Government has set up an online system to make it easier for us to chase bad payers. If they do not pay, then they should be threatened with Court action and a ruined credit history.

PS - I joined the UK Cabinet Office Small and Medium Sized Enterprise Panel in 2016. Several so-called business experts, including me, flagged up to the Government that paying a small company late can kill it. The Government took notice and decided to become exemplary payers. They targeted 85% of all payments within one month (and then later tightened this target). The Government made it mandatory for all Central Government departments to publish their payment statistics.

Guess what happened? The UK Government has always been better at paying bills on time than most countries governments. But once they started to measure and publish statistics on payment performance, they became an excellent payer.

WHY MORE SALES CAN ACTUALLY KILL YOUR BUSINESS

To help you understand the content of this story: I used to buy companies for a living. I have been involved in over 40 mergers and acquisitions. On average we bought one out of every 15 companies we looked at. Over 15 years we looked at over 500 companies.

One day the Corporate Finance advisor who used to find companies for me to look at was all excited. He was adamant that I had to go and see a company in the South of England. I was not sure I wanted to go but he was so excited I gave in. "This is the finest sales machine I have seen in many years - you will absolutely love it." The business was selling telephone systems to new startup companies, companies that were moving premises, or companies where the old phone system was just very old and unreliable.

When we walked in it was very loud. There was music blasting.

All the staff had earphones rather than desk-phones and rather than sit at desks; they were wandering around waving their arms and speaking very loudly down the microphone on the headset. Every time someone sold something, they walked over to a big brass bell and rang it loudly. It rang several times whilst we were watching.

I then sat down with the business owner to ask him about his business model. The business was already up for sale, so, either he thought it was worth a fortune and wanted to cash in, or, he was in financial trouble?

This small business had come from nowhere and become the largest, by volume, seller of phone systems for that manufacturer in under a year. It was a phenomenal achievement.

In the car park, as we left, the Corporate Finance Advisor asked me what I thought? He looked shocked when I said that the business would go bankrupt in six months. It went bankrupt in five and a half months, so I must have been feeling generous that day. Why? What happened and why was it so predictable?

To buy the phone system from the manufacturer cost many thousands of pounds. He was allowing customers to rent the phone system at a very small monthly payment (hence why they were selling so many). A quick calculation showed that it would be near the end of year three before he had received enough money from a customer to pay the manufacturer for the phone system. The more he sold, the more he owed the manufacturer.

This approach is fine if you raise a very large amount of money to finance the cash outflows in the first few years, but, he didn't. I asked a sneaky question - have you ever paid a bill on your personal credit card? He replied that of course he had as all new businessmen do. You only ever pay bills on your personal credit card when all other avenues of finance have been exhausted. It is ruinously expensive.

MY MESSAGE IS SIMPLE

If you think you will be selling a lot of something; then make sure you understand whether you are going to need a lot more cash (incremental working capital is the technical phrase) if it will take a while for each sale to get your money back. This man was what I call a 'shooting star' - people loved him for about a year and then he disappeared.

WHY SPREADSHEETS ARE LIKE WINE

It's on a spreadsheet so it must be true?

It never fails to amaze me how many people think that numbers must be true if they are on a spreadsheet.

The hardest thing to spot on a spreadsheet is something that is missing. Something that should be there that isn't. This is a genuine news article from 4th April 2018.

4th Apr 2018 - Conviviality, one of the UK's largest drinks wholesalers, is heading into administration after an emergency share issue failed to raise the £125m it needed.

The business has been in a death spiral since the beginning of March 2018, when the retailer said its adjusted EBITDA would be 20% lower than the £70m market expectation. The company later confirmed an expected range of adjusted EBITDA of £55.3m - £56.4m. £5.2m of that £14m came thanks to "a material error in the financial forecasts".

The error, it later admitted, was "a spreadsheet arithmetic error". The tumult didn't end there, though. Days later, Conviviality announced it hadn't budgeted for a £30m tax bill, due at the end of March.

The two profit shocks prompted a free fall which wiped out 60% of Conviviality's share value before trading was suspended by AIM on the 14th of March. The wholesale division of Conviviality was bought by C&C, the owners of Magners, in a pre-pack administration.

In December 2017, the value of Conviviality peaked at £747 million. Four months later it was worth virtually nothing.

Can you imagine this? A large company is running out of cash, so, they do a cash forecast to see how much money they have left? They only realised they had forgotten about the VAT bill when an invoice for £30m arrived and a very red-faced Finance Director had to call an emergency meeting of the Board to say that they didn't have enough cash to pay it. Within days they were in administration.

When something like this happens; it tells you that they have never done a cash forecast before. If they had done it before then they would have spotted the error in previous quarters because VAT bills come every three months.

MY MESSAGE IS SIMPLE

Spreadsheets are like wine; they get better over time.

As they are used, errors are found and gradually ironed out. Once a spreadsheet has been used regularly for several months it should have settled down.

THE PERFECT CASH FORECAST - REGULAR AND OFTEN

One of the big lessons from the Conviviality story is about how often you should do cash forecasts? Many people only do a formal cash forecast every few months. That only works in certain circumstances. Let's take a look ...

If you have been running a business for a long time and you know that each month follows a very predictable pattern of cash flow then you might be safe to leave it for a while so long as you keep an eye on the big quarterly payments for VAT and the annual payments for Corporation Tax.

Most businesses are not that predictable and if you do not do a regular cash flow forecast then you can end up with huge surprises like Conviviality did.

Regular and often is best.

We update our cash forecasts several times a month as we learn more information. The sooner you find a potential problem the longer you have to find a solution.

If you suddenly need money and urgently have to go to the bank to ask to borrow more money, do not be surprised if the bank will charge you more, as you are in no position to negotiate.

MY MESSAGE IS SIMPLE

Not everything in business is exciting. It is the boring stuff, like cash forecasts, that keep you alive. It is ok concentrating on trying to grow but staying alive as a business comes first. Just watch what the famous football managers do - they hire a great defence so that they stop losing games. Then they go on the attack.

LEARN FROM THE MARKET STALL

The market traders on the old-fashioned market stalls are some of the cleverest businesspeople I have seen. They, normally, haven't studied business in a classroom, they have been taught by their family or friends and we can learn a lot from looking more closely at how they operate.

They use their customers money wherever they can. What do I mean by that? They negotiate credit with their suppliers and then sell the goods quickly. They use the money they have collected from their customers to pay their suppliers' bills.

In every country around the world you see people setting up businesses with no money; as if by magic. There is no magic; they are simply using the same technique as the market traders.

This is the technique I used when I first set up AdEPT. I negotiated 90-day payment terms with our biggest supplier and then collected money from our customers by Direct Debit. We got paid in 14-days, but we didn't have to pay our suppliers until 76 days later. As you can imagine this reduced considerably the amount of money that I needed to start the business.

This is why we try to avoid holding stock whenever we can. If you hold stock for a long time; then you will end up paying the supplier before you have received any money from a customer.

MY MESSAGE IS SIMPLE

If you do not have a lot of money, then it teaches you to be inventive. Use your customers money wherever you can.

CROWD FUNDING - HOW NOT TO GIVE AWAY EQUITY

Recent years have seen a new way of raising cash: crowdfunding. But, is it new? Or, is it just a way of using technology to do things we have always done? I'm going to ignore the regulatory discussions about crowdfunding as some sites are regulated and others are not. With any new financial idea, the rules and regulations will probably tighten over time. In 2017, £217.7m was invested in UK crowdfunding platforms[12]. In 2015, the craft beer company Brewdog set a new world record for crowdfunding when it raised £19m.[13]

---

[12] Growth Business, 2018. *Top 10 crowdfunding platforms for businesses in 2018.* [online]. Available at: <https://www.growthbusiness.co.uk/top-10-crowdfunding-platforms-for-business-finance-2483726/> [Accessed on 30 November 2018]

[13] Brewdog, 2016. *Equity for Punks IV has closed.* [online]. Available at:

Crowdfunding is often seen as a way of getting ordinary people (as against City institutions) to invest in your business and buy a share. People back ideas they like, hence the popularity of Brewdog, a craft beer company. I'm not convinced that people understand that by paying £x for one share they are effectively valuing a startup very highly. So, this aspect of crowdfunding is very risky for the investor. To be honest, I don't want to get dragged into the pros and cons of buying a share of someone's company using crowdfunding.

Instead, I want to tell you a story about a smart way of using crowdfunding, without selling any ownership rights in your company. A friend wrote a humorous book and it was published by a well-known publisher. He was understandably very excited and proud about publishing his first book. Once it had been published for a while he started to think about the process. The sales of his book were good, compared to what he had expected, but by the time the publisher had taken their cut, he hadn't made lots of money from the enterprise. However, he loved the idea of publishing a second book. So, he decided to use Kickstarter. He wanted to cut out the publisher from the process and print the book himself. It obviously costs money if you want to produce a quality book and one of the big problems is how to decide the number of books to print? If you print too many and they do not sell; then you could lose money on the book.

He produced a humorous video and explained what he wanted to do in rap. The video went viral and lots of people wanted to join in. Instead of selling part of his company, he offered a variety of 'packages'. Depending upon how much you invested dictated what you received in return. I can't remember every package so I will give you a flavour of the idea. The smaller package gave you an autographed copy of the book. A higher investment gave you a signed book and an invitation to the book launch party. Invest even more and you could have dinner, or a day out with the author. He was massively oversubscribed, and the book was printed with a bigger run than expected. For a humorous author, he was a far better businessman than he appreciated (or would accept).

MY MESSAGE IS SIMPLE

This approach is a modern alternative to the market stall concept we discussed earlier - use your customers money wherever possible. He had found a way of removing the risk from the whole venture and using this process, he made more money. Modern technology often helps you to do old ideas and concepts in a quicker and easier way. Why are we surprised that raising money would be any different?

<https://www.brewdog.com/blog/equity-for-punks-iv-has-closed> [Accessed on 1 November 2019]

CHAPTER TWO
Selling Profitably

THE ECONOMICS OF ONE

In this section we will look at how to sell and make a profit. But surely that is obvious I hear you say? No; unfortunately, people make lots of mistakes when they are selling, and I will try to give you some help and tips where I can. If you cannot sell, then you will not survive. However, even if you do sell it does not necessarily mean you will be successful.

Let's take a look at what I call 'The Economics of One'.

Before you try to sell a thousand of something, ask yourself whether you fully understand the cost of selling just one? If you lose money selling one; then you will lose a lot of money selling a thousand; unless there are some clear economies of scale.

Let's look at an example.

A fashion company bought a man's suit for £100. Sales were slow so it decided to clear out its' stock ready to prepare for next season's offerings. The man's suit was put up for sale at £100 just to get rid of it. What is wrong with that? If the £100 we paid the supplier for the suit was the cost before tax; then we have a big problem as the £100 we received from our customer was actually £83.33 plus 20% VAT. We have just lost £16.67 on that suit. Not so bad if you only sell one but a complete disaster if you sell large volumes.

I used sales tax in that example, but I could have used delivery costs and showed that the real cost was more than £100. Unfortunately, in business the devil is very much in the detail. And by the way - if you wrapped the suit in a large gift bag and gave the customer a free suit carrier please ensure you include those costs as well. I hope you see my point.

MY MESSAGE IS SIMPLE

Spend a lot of time building a clear picture of every cost associated with your products and the margins you make from various selling prices (because selling prices change). How many items will you have to sell to recover the overhead costs of the business such as the office building and your staff? Be honest with yourself: can you realistically expect to sell more than that quantity so that you actually make a profit?

Unless you understand the economics of selling one be wary of selling lots of something. If you think your costs will drop if you can buy bigger quantities; then get quotes for those volumes: do not guess the impact of volume buying as most people overestimate how much they can save.

WHICH MAKES MORE MONEY - CAFES OR RESTAURANTS?

One of the potential problems with selling is that most people fall into the 'glamour trap'. Ask people whether they would like to open a restaurant, or a cafe and they often choose a restaurant because it seems more glamorous. Others choose a restaurant because the price of an expensive meal with wine is much more than the humble cup of tea or coffee.

The reality is that many cafes are much more profitable than restaurants.

Many restaurants have heavy costs; often typified by the cost of linen tablecloths and napkins being cleaned after every meal. Their biggest problem is often the number of meals, or covers, they can serve. Many can only serve one meal per seat (or cover) at lunch and a maximum of two meals in the evening. Given that most restaurants are not full at lunchtime and many evenings in the week, there is a limit to how many meals they can provide each week.

A cafe in contrast is open all day and whilst some of the items they serve are relatively cheap, they are also very profitable. A good example is tea or coffee where the margin can be about 95% or even higher. If you can make, say, £2.75 on every cup of coffee then that quickly mounts up.

The key in a cafe is how many times in a day each seat (or cover) is used. In a restaurant a cover might only be used once a day, but in a cafe, it could be constant for the peak parts of the day.

MY MESSAGE IS SIMPLE

Do not fall for selling the 'glamorous' products and services. Instead concentrate on selling those that make most money. You should be aware of the volumes you are likely to sell. The more you can use your infrastructure, in this example: tables and chairs, the better.

BEWARE OF USING THE WRONG NUMBER

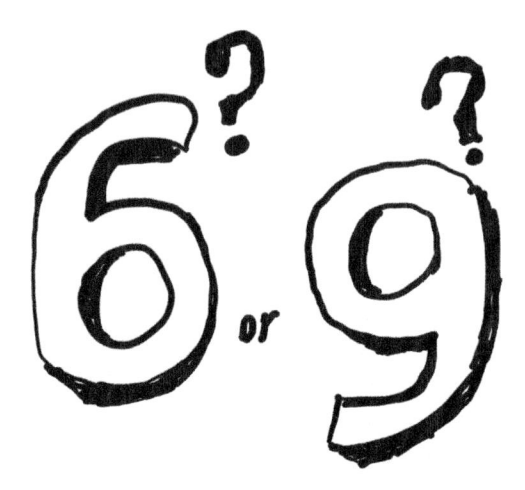

When deciding what to charge customers many companies do it by adding a certain amount to the cost of a product. Let's imagine you buy something for £100. Some people add a 'markup' to the cost. Let's use 50% as an example. A 50% markup on something that costs £100 means that you will sell the item for £150.

What is wrong with that you might ask?

It depends on how much money you want to make. My worry is that many people fool themselves into thinking they are making 50% margins and they are not. Let's take another look at the same example.

You are selling for £150 and it cost you £100 so you are making £50 margin. The margin on sales is 50/150 = 33%.

You should always express your margins as 'margin as a percentage of sales'. This will give you a smaller number than markup (33% v 50%) and it stops you fooling yourself about how much money you are making.

Sales taxes; VAT in the UK, can make this much worse.

If you are selling a product to a consumer then by law the price must include all taxes; VAT in the UK. At the time of writing (2019) VAT in the UK was 20%. Let's assume that the product we discussed was sold to a consumer. The profitability suddenly looks very different.

20% of the £150 (ie £30) goes to the taxman. Your margin is no longer £50 it is £20 and your sales price, excluding sales taxes is £120. Your margins are now 20/120 = 16.7%.

We started by deciding we would add 50% markup to the cost of a product. This sounded like we were going to make huge profits. We then realised that whilst this initially sounded great, once VAT had been taken into account the margins were only 16.7% on sales.

MY MESSAGE IS SIMPLE

This is a really important lesson.

Do not use the wrong number when calculating margins. You must look at margins as a percentage of sales revenue excluding sales taxes. Do not forget sales taxes and that this margin needs to pay for all of the other costs of the business: wages, premises etc.

For the accountants amongst you - I assumed that the £100 purchase price was excluding VAT.

HOW TO USE PAGE 3 PRICING

Condition 7:

Hammers do not come with handles.

Handles £12 extra

PRICE LIST | Page 3

There are many products that appear to be inexpensive, but in reality, are not. It does not seem obvious how that product or service makes its' money. I call this phenomenon 'page 3 pricing'.

What I mean by page 3 pricing is this: if you can be bothered to read the full price list then somewhere buried in the detail will be the clause that explains how the product makes money. It is rarely on the first page; hence why I call this 'page 3 pricing'.

Let's take a look at some examples.

Buying a printer for your PC or laptop is relatively inexpensive. The manufacturers are almost willing to give them away at a loss so that they can make their money on selling you expensive toner cartridges.

Electrical items such as washing machines and TV's are low profit items unless you take the 'extended warranty option'. Your TV will now be fixed if it breaks over the next 5 years. The TV retailers can see the statistics: TV's do not tend to break down and as new technology is constantly issued many people replace their TV before the 5 years is up. You are therefore paying for something that you are very unlikely to use.

The price to hire a car on the internet can be extremely low. However, when you get to the rental office where you pick up the car, you are often faced with huge insurance charges that cost more than the car rental itself. This is one example where the 'page 3' element is now so big that I would not be surprised if legislation is introduced to ban the practice. That is what happened with airline ticket prices when they went too far in advertising cheap flights that bore no relation to the price you ended up paying. The various add-on options for flights are now much more obvious with clearly identified costs for putting bags in the hold, carrying golf clubs, choosing your seat etc.

Most mobile phone bundles include a set volume of texts, data usage etc. Few people ever use their monthly allowance, so most people are paying for stuff they do not use, just to get the peace of mind of a set monthly charge.

There are several lessons here.

Some customers prefer the certainty of a fixed monthly charge than the worry of an occasional high unexpected bill. The key clause is that if you do not use your allowance in the month then you lose them; you cannot carry the unused amount into next month. Note that the clause here is sometimes even harder to spot as it may be in the contract terms and conditions rather than the price list.

MY MESSAGE IS SIMPLE

Your headline pricing needs to be competitive or you will not sell very much. You are a business, so you need to make profit somewhere. Think about what your version of page 3 pricing is, but, do not push it so far that customers (and potentially regulators) will hate you for it.

HOW TO ENCOURAGE PEOPLE TO BUY MORE PRODUCTS

There are all sorts of different ways to get users to buy more of your products. We are going to take a look at a few. The objective of this section is to make you think about whether these techniques work for your kind of product as they do not work for everything.

There is a famous quote from Mr. Colman of Colman's Mustard fame - "I don't make my money from what my customers eat. I make money from what they leave on the plate." Almost everyone puts mustard on a plate and then leaves some. Is that an accident? I don't think so. The mustard jar is not designed to make it easy to dispense very small quantities. It has a wide neck so that you can get a knife or spoon into the jar.

Some toothpaste manufacturers have gradually increased the size of the hole at the end of a toothpaste tube so that it dispenses a larger amount when you squeeze it.

Many modern drinks products have much wider necks on the bottle so that you can drink it easier and quicker.

Relatively few companies sell foodstuffs in small enough quantities for just one person to eat. This might start to change as a larger percentage of the population is living on their own, but there is no real incentive for manufacturers to sell less.

Whenever the Government has tried to regulate foodstuffs; to reduce obesity by cutting portion sizes, the price has not dropped as much as the size, so the supplier often makes more money on the product. As an example - a chocolate bar may now be 20% smaller, but the price only fell 10%.

Buy one get one free is increasingly common, but in foodstuffs it simply increases waste. Giving most people two bags of salad leaves rather than one simply guarantees more food is thrown away. At the point of sale, it feels like a bargain even though it is not.

Does this approach just apply to foodstuffs? No. Most mobile phones come with bundles of minutes or texts. As we discussed previously: very few people use anywhere near their full monthly allowance, so they are paying a fixed monthly rental for stuff they do not use.

One of the great success stories in business is Apple. Let's take a look at how they sell iPhones. They always launch several versions of each iPhone. I'm not referring to different colours. We are going to look at the storage options. In February 2020 there were three options for storage on the iPhone: 64GB (£729), 128Gb (£779) and 256Gb (£879). A salesperson simply needs to explain that photos and videos take up space, so you might need more storage. Extra storage does not cost a lot to manufacture, but as we can see the price difference between 64GB and 256GB is £150. They are trying to persuade you that you would be safer buying extra storage (even if you have no idea whether you will need it) because this is presumably their most profitable version of the product.

IBM have for many years pre-installed optional software features that you cannot unlock and use without paying a supplementary fee.

MY MESSAGE IS SIMPLE

Selling more is not simply about doing more sales. It also needs you to think about how your product or service is consumed or used.

A DISASTER WAITING TO HAPPEN

The UK Government decided that the small number of very large energy companies in the UK were charging too much, and the sector would benefit from increased competition from smaller companies. As normally happens when a sector deregulates a range of competitors quickly sprang up. After having a close look at the industry, we decided not to join in.

In November 2016, GB Energy, one of the new challenger companies based in Preston, went into liquidation with 160,000 customers not knowing what would happen to their energy supply.[14] Surely, they were doing well. They had grown to 160,000 customers so quickly. Obviously not. What went

---

[14] Joe Malinowski, 25 June 2019. *GB Energy supply ... how did it happen and what happens next?* [online]. Available at <https://www.theenergyshop.com/articles/gb-energy-supply-what-happens-next> [Accessed on 9 February 2020]

wrong?

The disaster was highly predictable.

GB Energy was selling 3-year contracts to customers with fixed prices. However, they didn't sign a fixed price 3-year agreement with a supplier. They were buying energy on the 'spot' market where you can only buy enough energy for the next few weeks. All went well so long as 'spot' prices were low but when energy prices rose 35-40% within a matter of weeks every single customer contract became loss-making and they ran out of money extremely fast.

Another energy company, Future Energy, went bankrupt in January 2018 with 10,000 customers not knowing what would happen to their energy supply.[15] Their issue was similar but slightly different: they couldn't get the same volume discounts from suppliers as their giant competitors, so, when the larger competitors started to reduce their prices to beat the new competitors, they could not compete.

In the period November 2016 to September 2019, fourteen energy companies went bankrupt.[16] Nine more were believed to be in trouble.

In the UK Telecoms market companies can compete against the likes of BT because they operate in a regulated industry. OFCOM mandates that Openreach cannot give volume discounts so all competitors buy at the same cost as BT. Equally as important: the prices are often fixed for the contract period. It is sometimes even better than that because some costs are being gradually regulated down.

MY MESSAGE IS SIMPLE

Do not sell long-term contracts to customers on a fixed price basis unless you have a long-term supply agreement at fixed (or reducing) prices. Your costs and margins must be predictable. If sales volumes change then costs must change in line. Beware of contracts with large set-up costs. Your profitability could change rapidly as sales volumes vary.

---

[15] Adam Vaughan, 25 Jan 2018. *Customers urged not to switch supply after Future Energy collapse.* [online]. Available at <https://www.theguardian.com/money/2018/jan/25/customers-urged-not-to-switch-supply-after-future-energy-collapse> [Accessed on 9 February 2020]

[16] Sam Meadows. 6 Sep 2019. *Energy firm with upfront fees goes bust prompting fears over large customer debts.* [online]. Available at <https://www.telegraph.co.uk/bills-and-utilities/gas-electric/energy-firm-upfront-fees-goes-bust-prompting-fears-large-customer/> [Accessed on 9 February 2020]

THERE IS NO SUCH THING AS A SEXY POUND

Earlier in the book I talked about the problem of everyone wanting to sell the 'glamorous products.' I come from the technology industry and most salespeople seem to want to sell complex solutions rather than simple straightforward stuff.

One of the sales guys that worked for me was the opposite. If he saw a simple opportunity, then he would find a way of selling and making some money.

He was in a chain of pub restaurants one day and watched the young waiters and waitresses taking orders on iPads (or a similar tablet device). He went to talk to the manager. Here are some of the simple questions he asked:

- Do people lose or steal the iPads?

- Are they always charged and ready to last a full shift as you do not have any other way to take orders?
- Where do you store them at night?
- What happens if the manager takes home the key to the cupboard and then does not turn in the day after because he is sick?

A modern high-tech solution to what used to be very simple - writing down your order on a notepad - had become a logistical nightmare.

The salesman commissioned a metal storage locker with lots of charging points in the back. Instead of a physical lock with a key, the locker was secured by a PIN number so that others could open it if needed. The pub restaurant chain ordered one for every site they owned.

MY MESSAGE IS SIMPLE

We are in business to make money. A pound is a pound - there is no such thing as a sexy pound.

THE PROBLEM WITH ENTERPRISE CUSTOMERS

In all industries selling to businesses rather than consumers, the market can be split into three sections: small business customers, medium-sized business customers and enterprise customers.

My company, quite deliberately, concentrated on selling to small and medium-sized businesses. Why is that? Partly it is because if we tried to sell to very large customers then we would be competing for work against the huge companies, but that is not the main reason.

When you are selling to small and medium sized customers, you end up, often after much discussion, with a shopping list of what they want to buy. This means that you know exactly what your selling price is, but more importantly, you also know the cost of what you are to supply and the margin you are going to make. The items you are selling are normally standard products where you know the cost of them.

When you sell to enterprise customers you know exactly what the selling price is, but you sometimes do not know exactly what your costs are as there is often a bespoke element that involves items such as development. These types of costs are hard to estimate precisely.

Do we see examples of companies getting themselves into problems by selling to enterprise customers? Yes, particularly in the technology sector where software development is sometimes involved. BT had huge problems with large contracts at BT Global Services. As long ago as 2009, Robert Peston of the BBC said, "What's gone wrong at Global Services - which managed IT and communications for giant organisations like Reuters, the NHS and Microsoft - is that costs have spiraled out of control. One NHS contract has been particularly horrid - and is responsible for a huge chunk of a £1.3 billion one-off debit for sorting out loss-making contracts".[17]

MY MESSAGE IS SIMPLE

Stick to contracts where you can predict the margins. If you do have to enter a contract with a development element; then ensure it is a tiny proportion of your overall turnover. Wherever possible, share the risk with the customer by charging time and materials on a daily basis.

I suppose I am saying learn to walk before you run. If you get big enough then eventually you will need to learn how to sell to enterprise customers - just don't do it straight away.

---

[17] Robert Peston, 14 May 2009. *BT: Self-inflicted wounds.* [online]. Available at <https://www.bbc.co.uk/blogs/thereporters/robertpeston/2009/05/bt_selfinflicted_wounds.html> Accessed on 5 March 2020.

WHERE SHOULD THE MANAGING DIRECTOR SIT?

The number of buildings you have and how they are laid out has a huge impact on managing a business. The easiest way to run a business (and my strong preference) is to have the entire organisation in one building in one primarily open plan office. You can sense what is happening in the company by simply walking around and listening. You will instinctively start to spot any tensions between departments and individual members of staff.

What do you try to avoid? In one job they gave me an office on a floor of executive directors. Unless I made a conscious effort to go to another floor in the building, I could go for hours without seeing another member of staff; this is a complete disaster. You need to be close to the staff and chat to them regularly.

If you have a single building with several floors or wings, then try to sit near the sales team. I am not anti-Operations, Finance or any other department. I simply recognise that you can control the major overhead costs if you watch recruitment. The cost of most support functions does not change regularly. If your costs are fairly fixed, then your results will succeed or fail depending on how much you sell.

You will very quickly learn to sense whether the Sales team are doing well or having a hard time.

When you run a Group you inevitably have several buildings. Do not underestimate how big a challenge this poses. I always used to host Finance meetings at the site. This meant that I knew I had to visit that site at least once a month. I wanted to chat to people and for them to know me and be happy to approach me. There is no point pretending this is easy and it will work with every member of staff because it won't. However, there is a lot to be said for simply being seen to be there and care.

MY MESSAGE IS SIMPLE

You need to be close to your Sales team. Sales are the lifeblood of any business.

GOOD NEWS TRAVELS FAST

I generally know whether we are going to have a great sales meeting even before I enter the room, or, have seen any figures. How is that possible? Am I some kind of psychic? No.

'Good news travels fast'. If we win something unusually large, then people cannot help sharing the good news. Texts, emails and excited phone calls will happen very quickly. And let us not forget 'success has many fathers' (and 'failure is an orphan').

The corollary of this is **'bad news travels slowly'**. That is why if there is a surprise in a meeting, it is often bad news, because people have been putting off sharing it.

I fully accept this is a generalisation and some of you will argue you are not guilty of this. My simple response is that some things change, but human nature doesn't. This has been my experience for nearly 30 years as a boss.

MY MESSAGE IS SIMPLE

Good news and bad news should be shared as soon as it happens. No-one likes unexpected surprises in the middle of a meeting.

Craig Wilson is one of the most senior IT people in the UK. He was CEO of EDS UK, HP Enterprise, Xchanging and CSC. He has managed many thousands of people. When I told him this story; he laughed. He said that he recognised this trait in sales meetings, so he had always tried to have a good surprise - Craig calls it "Always have a Snickers in your sock".

SALESPEOPLE HAVE TO COVER THEIR OWN COSTS

It costs a lot of money to pay a sales force. Not only does a salesperson want a basic salary; they often also need cars, laptops and mobile phones.

Most decent salespeople should be able to do a good interview, so they are often impressive when you first meet them. However, this does not guarantee that they will sell anything. It is very difficult to tell in advance which salespeople will make you any money.

The first job of a salesperson is to sell enough products or services for the margin generated to cover their own costs (and do not forget payroll taxes - National Insurance in the UK).

Let's do an example:

Let's imagine that the basic pay of a salesperson is £3,000 per month. Payroll tax (national insurance in the UK) is 13.8% = £414. The lease for the company car is £500 per month and another £500 is spent on petrol. Their mobile phone bill is £50 per month. They also need a £1,000 laptop. If we spread the cost over 36 months' then this is another £28 per month.

The total cost of this salesperson, before they earn any commission is £4,492.

The important point here is that we are discussing margin not sales revenue. If a salesperson sells a widget for £100 but we have to buy the widget for £90 then the margin is only £10.

Many sales commissions give the salesperson a portion of the margin (often around 10%). This means that if the widget above makes £10 margin then the salesperson keeps £1 as commission so the net margin is £9.

If the salesperson costs £4,492 per month then they will need to sell 4,492/9 = 499 widgets just to cover their own costs.

Only when they sell 500 widgets, or more does that salesperson generate any money for the company.

MY MESSAGE IS SIMPLE

If a salesperson cannot sell enough to cover their own cost, then you are better off not having them as they are losing you money every month. You need to understand what each salesperson is costing you and what they need to sell to make it worthwhile keeping them.

I used to review this on a rolling 3-month basis as all salespeople have great months, poor months and average months.

BEWARE OF CREATING AN ACCIDENTAL FRANKENSTEIN

An 'Accidental Frankenstein' is when you create a monster without realising what you were doing.

You need to be very careful when you create commission schemes for salespeople. There is a real danger that you look at the idea and do not think about what that scheme will look like in say five-years-time.

Let me share a true story but I won't name the people as that is not fair.

One of my companies recognised that we needed to keep customers as well as winning new ones. They therefore decided to incentivise the salesman who originally won that customer to keep them for as many years as possible. This meant that the sales team were paid part of their commission for a new sale and part of their commission for keeping customers.

What is wrong with this? Nothing if you have thought it through properly.

Not surprisingly, 10 years later, the highest earning salespeople were the ones who had been with the company longest.

When we ranked 250 Group employees in salary order it became clear that the main salesman at one of our smallest companies was the 3rd highest paid person in the entire group. To make things worse, he earned so much from his existing customers, that he didn't sell much to new people anymore.

We had created a commission scheme that not only overpaid people, it also incentivised them not to bother selling anymore.

Any commission scheme should not be included in the employment contract. The employment contract should simply refer to a commission scheme. This allows you to reissue the sales commission as and when you need.

You should also be careful about the timing of when you pay the commissions. Wherever possible you should only pay the salesperson when the customer pays you. This avoids you paying out money early and therefore needing more cash to run your business. It also avoids problems when customers do not pay, and you need to 'claw back' commissions.

MY MESSAGE IS SIMPLE

Spend a long time thinking about your proposed commission scheme for salespeople. Monitor it regularly to ensure you are getting the results you expected and there are no unforeseen consequences. Think about what the commission scheme will look like, in say, three-years-time.

Beware of creating an 'Accidental Frankenstein'.

CONSIDER SUCCESS-ONLY SELLING

How do you reduce the risk of spending a lot of money on a sales force with no guaranteed return?

For many years I used an approach called 'success only selling'.

I sought other businesses who sold similar products to mine, but not the actual ones I sold. I then offered them the chance to increase their product range by selling my products alongside their own. When they sold something, I gave them a share of the profit (or margin).

This meant that I only ever paid out money if a partner sold something. If I had hired salespeople, I may have been paying them even if they had sold nothing or very little.

MY MESSAGE IS SIMPLE

There are lots of different ways of selling products and services. Hiring salespeople is just one option. In certain circumstances it is the right way to sell, but not always.

If you do decide to sell through a 'partner channel' then you have to be very clear about how they interact with your own internal sales force. You do not want two sales channels competing for the same potential customers as they will simply drive the price down and cause huge conflict.

The most common way of solving this dilemma is that a partner registers an opportunity when they find it. The direct sales force is then told to leave that customer alone. The problem with this is that it involves tremendous trust from both parties. As soon as that trust is broken, you will never get it back and do not forget that partners talk to each other, so word will quickly spread that your partner management team cannot be trusted.

WHO SHOULD SELECT SUPPLIERS?

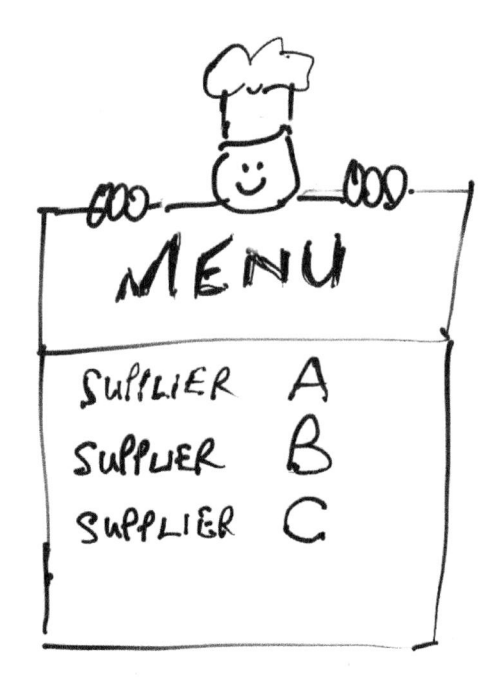

We incentivise sales teams to sell as much as possible. That is what we measure. Let us not be surprised therefore that they hate turning down a potential sale.

What is wrong with that?

If the potential sale involves something that we don't normally do and needs a new supplier, we should be very careful.

Salespeople should not be allowed to appoint new suppliers, without the agreement of other functions. Often the final decision to appoint a new supplier is given to someone outside of the sales department. Why is this?

There must be a discussion with the Operations team who will be left to clean up the mess.

Do we know how to:

- Provision the service?
- Install it?
- Fix a fault?
- Do moves and changes?
- Terminate a contract and facilitate a transfer to a competitor if we lose the business?

Operations must be allowed to vet new suppliers even if it upsets the sales team in the short term.

MY MESSAGE IS SIMPLE

We must seek to use a small number of suppliers and become expert at their products and services. Having lots of suppliers with only 1 or 2 customers is a day-to-day support nightmare.

In the Product Development section, we will look in more detail at how to select suppliers.

HOW DO YOU GET ECONOMIES OF SCALE IN SUPPORT COSTS?

Let's split products and services into two types: simple ones where you deliver the product and then that is the end of the sale and more complex ones where you have to support the product throughout the life of the contract or product guarantee.

In general, complex products and services need a call centre to provide support and this is when it gets tricky to work out product profitability.

You typically have to support the product or service through every aspect of its' lifecycle: installation, payments, faults, moves and changes and eventually termination. Let's look at some typical queries for a service like broadband:

Installation

- I have tried to install the broadband router as per the instructions, but I still cannot get access to the internet - can you help me please?

Payments

- My direct debit bounced so you have sent me a late payment letter. Can I pay over the phone?

Faults

- My wifi doesn't work. How do I fix it?

Moves and changes

- I signed a two-year contract. I am moving house and I still have nine months to go on my contract. What happens? Can I take my service with me?

Termination

- I have found another supplier cheaper than you, so I want to leave. What do I need to do to stop your monthly bills?

I am sure that you can think of many other products or services that need a support Helpdesk where customers can ring for advice or help when they have problems.

My Chairman for over a decade, Roger Wilson, used to say, "There is no shortage of revenue in our industry - there is billions of pounds of it. The problem is that there is too much cost supporting that revenue."

What did he mean by that? What is the problem?

When you are setting up a Helpdesk you need at least two people, even if you are only covering office hours, Monday to Friday. People have lunches and holidays and are occasionally sick. It therefore isn't possible to run a Helpdesk with only one person.

When you launch a new product, you need to hire two people for the Helpdesk even though you have no customers. Let's use a fault desk as an example.

If a product only has a fault on average once a year, then you can only expect a call from that customer once a year. You therefore need a lot of customers to keep two people busy on a Helpdesk. Let's take a closer look at the mathematics.

Let's imagine one person can comfortably handle 10 fault calls a day. With the minimum two people you can handle 20 fault calls a day. The working year in the UK is about 226 days after you remove holidays, bank holidays and weekends. That means that two people can handle 226 x 20 customers = 4,520 customers in a year.

When you launch a new product or service it will probably take you a long time to get to 4,520 customers, so until you reach that point, you are paying too much for your Helpdesk staff.

You either need to find a way of getting more customers quickly, to achieve economies of scale, or you need to create multi-skilled jobs where the Helpdesk staff have something else to do when they have no faults to deal with.

We talked previously about understanding the true cost of the product or service you sell. This is where it gets complex. How do you decide what the support cost per product is?

If you need two members of staff, then you will need to spread their cost over the products you expect to sell - the key question is - how many products do you expect to sell? Do you spread the cost of the two people over say 5,000 units or 1,000 units?

If you spread the cost over too few units then the cost of support will be very high, and you are in danger of pricing yourself too high in the marketplace. However, if you assume you are going to sell very high volumes and therefore the support cost per unit is very small, you run the risk of not selling enough to cover your costs. The only way to crack this 'chicken and egg' problem is to make a sensible guess on sales volumes, but to then review progress constantly.

I explained earlier that I have looked at several hundred companies over the last decade and it never ceases to amaze me how many simply do not understand which of their products and services actually lose money.

The most common reason for loss-making products is that you simply do not sell enough volume to cover the support cost.

MY MESSAGE IS SIMPLE

If you are in a business that needs a Helpdesk then, you must be very clear how you are going to create economies of scale or multi-skilled jobs, as you run the risk of making very little money. It is no accident that bigger companies are sometimes more profitable.

Small companies often find it difficult to find lots of new customers. They, perhaps understandably, concentrate on selling as many products and services as possible to their existing customers. The problem is that some small companies sometimes make the mistake of launching products when they do not understand the cost of supporting them.

Having lots of products, with a small number of customers for each product, costs a fortune in support.

CHAPTER THREE
People

THE MOST IMPORTANT THING - RESPECT

I sometimes listen to Ted's Talks when I am walking. I listened to an interesting one, from Christine Porath.[18] A team of researchers had done a study on what employees want most at work. They wanted to understand whether it was different around the world.

The first, perhaps surprising, answer was that it does not vary around the world. In places as diverse as Japan, USA, Europe or Africa the top answer was always the same.

---

[18] Christine Porath, Tedx Talks 2018. *Why being respectful to your coworkers is good for business.* [online] Available at
<https://www.ted.com/talks/christine_porath_why_being_respectful_to_your_coworkers_is_good_for_business?language=en#t-691304> [Accessed on 3rd February 2020]

The people who launched the study expected 'decent pay' or 'promotion prospects' to be the most important things that people wanted when they went to work. Whilst they are important, they are not top of the list. Regardless of what level you are in an organisation, the answer was 'respect'.

"I want my boss to respect me."

"I want my work colleagues to treat me with respect."

This is not just an important lesson for management, it is important for everyone. If you do not treat your co-workers with respect, then do not be surprised if they do not return it.

Respect also has an impact on motivation. As Sheryl Sandberg, COO of Facebook put it, "Motivation comes from working on things we care about. It also comes from working with people we care about."[19]

I asked a new starter how they felt after six weeks with the company. The answer has stayed with me. "I love it here. It feels like I have joined a family. Everyone is so friendly that I love going to work".

MY MESSAGE IS SIMPLE

Treat people the way you would like to be treated yourself.

---

[19] Sheryl Sandberg, Nell Scovell 2013. *Lean In: Women, Work, and the Will to Lead.* Knopf

HATS - HIRE ATTITUDE, TRAIN SKILL

I sometimes think that we approach recruitment all wrong.

The most common way to recruit someone is to make a long list of all the technical skills you need and then to search through CV's to find the best match to the list.

Always try to interview at least two candidates. Let's imagine that the first candidate has ticked every technical skill we are looking for. The second candidate only has half of the skills we are looking for.

At the interview it becomes clear that the highly skilled candidate has a grumpy, miserable personality, but the one with fewer skills is bubbling with enthusiasm.

Now pause for a second and look at the people close to your desk. How many of them have been with the business for two years or more? The normal answer is most; because many people stay with jobs for quite a while. Who do you want to sit near for the next four or five years? A grumpy constantly moaning person or someone who has infectious enthusiasm? The enthusiastic person needs a lot more looking after in the early years, as they need training, but their impact on the morale of the team will be huge.

MY MESSAGE IS SIMPLE

You can't change someone's personality, but you can change their skillset.

HATS - Hire Attitude Train Skill

HOW TO SET TARGETS

When people are new to management, they are understandably keen to impress. I sometimes see people suggesting that they can do things that do not seem realistic. It is easy to sit there and simply say, "That sounds great. Please get on with it." But what is the point? If you know in your heart that it is simply a matter of time before they come back and admit they have failed to achieve what they promised.

The old saying. "an old head on young shoulders" has stood the test of time for good reasons.

My advice to anyone asked to set budgets or targets is this.

- Work out the number you are comfortable to achieve.

- Reduce it by 10%. This reduced number is the number you should share with senior management as things can go wrong and if they do not go wrong, then you have a chance of beating your target number.

- Add 25% to the timescale. It is rare that things can be done quicker than you think. It is much more common to find that the task is more difficult than you think. This can be because you have forgotten something, but it is often because you are dependent on someone else doing their bit. Just because a task is of high importance to you, does not mean that it is of a high importance to the other person. They may have a big list of tasks before they get to yours. This is even more pronounced when the person you are dependent on works for another company with a different boss with different priorities.

MY MESSAGE IS SIMPLE

Under promise and over deliver.

WHAT CAN WE LEARN FROM ALEX FERGUSON?

I am not a Manchester United fan, but I do recognise that Sir Alex Ferguson's record as a manager will probably never be equaled. He managed the football team for 27 years from 1986 to 2013. In that time, he won 38 trophies, including 13 Premier League and 2 UEFA Champions League titles.

Let's see what we can learn from him.

He doesn't play centre forwards in goal. Come on - that is obvious? Is it? The UK Government reshuffles its ministers every 12 months or so. As soon as they get the hang of a department they get moved. Would a business ever move the Finance Director to run the sales team and the Sales Director to run Human Resources? That is effectively what the Government sometimes does.

In business it is a bit more subtle. People get promoted into positions they never planned. How many people look at their career and think, "How did I end up here?"

Sir Alex played people in their best position. Take a look at your senior team and consider whether they are doing their most appropriate role. Good people can easily be ruined by simply playing them in the wrong position.

Paul Pogba is one of the world's best players but when he first went to Man Utd he struggled. He is arguably better at attacking than defending and he was being asked to do something which didn't come naturally to him. The answer (I think) was to hire Matic, a defensive midfielder. Matic concentrated on the defending and this allowed Pogba to attack more without worrying about what happened behind him.

What has this got to do with business?

Sometimes you have to hire an 'enabler' so that you can get the best out of someone. I have seen many salespeople struggle with spreadsheets and take ages to put proposals and quotes together. Hiring a commercial person who can do the 'boring numbers bit' allows the best salespeople to do what they do best - talk to people and sell.

MY MESSAGE IS SIMPLE

Play to people's strengths. Praise them for what they are good at and hire someone else to fill their skill gaps.

I LIKE ME, LET'S GET ANOTHER ONE

When you get promoted to senior management you have clearly had a very good career and some success along the way. The danger is that you start to believe that the skills that got you to that position are more of what your company needs. Sometimes that is true but not always.

When you are recruiting there is always a danger of unconscious bias towards someone who has the same skills as yourself. These people are easier to recognise.

When recruiting be very clear what problem you are trying to solve. If you watch children picking a football team, they will have 11 attackers if you let them, when what you need is a balanced team and at least one goalkeeper.

MY MESSAGE IS SIMPLE

Never recruit in your own image. You will end up with more of your strengths and you won't have fixed any of your weaknesses. Understand your skills gap and fill it.

GETTING IT WRONG WHEN HIRING

Let's be honest; recruiting the right people is really difficult. Some people come across great in interviews but then turn out to be rather different. In this section I'm not going to cover interviews and selection. Instead I am going to look at the more practical issue of what you do when you have hired the wrong person?

I made it a standard part of our employment offers that every hire was on a three-month probation when they started. This was regardless of rank in the organisation. This allows you to get rid of people if you have made a big mistake.

However, let's not get carried away - you cannot simply do what you want - you need to set expectations for all new starters. What proficiency level are they meant to achieve by the end of the three-month probation period?

We often used to extend a probation period and give the employee a Personal Improvement Plan if we thought they had a chance of making it given a little longer with clear training and objectives.

If you let someone go, then you will find that your team will thank you. They are the ones who will have to fix a team member's mistakes and put up with their grumpy moods. Often, they are relieved that you have taken a decision that will help them.

The big caveat is this: so long as you treated the person you are letting go with dignity. If you treat a leaver badly then your team will remember it forever, and rightly so.

MY MESSAGE IS SIMPLE

You are never going to get every recruitment right. Don't beat yourself up about it. Use probationary periods in employment offers as a quick way of fixing mistakes when you make them. Bite the bullet early. If someone does not fit with your organisation then it rarely gets better over time.

THE PROBLEM OF SHORT ATTENTION SPANS

I have never been a big fan of anything that happens once a year. Let's take a look at bonuses and appraisals.

I much prefer monthly bonuses to annual bonuses. The problem with giving someone an annual bonus target is that they quickly forget the details of how the bonus works. It is also difficult to create an annual bonus that entirely depends upon that individuals' performance. More often than not, annual bonuses involve team, or even company, targets. The individual often loses sight of how they can influence the result.

If you publish the results regularly, let's say monthly, it only helps a bit. If you are way off target by say month four or five, then no-one will be motivated towards that bonus for the next seven or eight months.

I prefer monthly bonus schemes where the targets can be changed as required. If you have a multi-skilled team then you can change the target according to the latest problem that you are trying to solve. Let's say the problem at the start of the year is the speed at which staff are answering the phone to customers and later in the year you need to improve debt collection. The ability to tell staff at the start of each month what this months' target is and why, is hugely powerful.

Let's look at another example. Imagine that my boss thinks I am not very good at something. What is the point waiting nearly a year until my next appraisal to tell me how I need to improve?

Try to tie monthly bonuses to monthly feedback explaining why the person earned the bonus amount they did and how they could improve and earn more money next month. This gives regular feedback and improves performance very quickly.

MY MESSAGE IS SIMPLE

People have a short attention span. Use monthly bonus schemes and monthly feedback to improve performance rapidly.

NO NEGS ON MY TEAM

I ran one business that had seven regional sales managers. I wasn't sure what I thought of one of the regional sales managers, so I asked if I could go to one of his sales team meetings.

My doubts about him vanished in a few minutes.

He had a limp and walked with a stick. Never make the mistake of thinking that someone with a physical difficulty does not have a sharp mind. He gathered his team in a circle and then stood up to talk. He said something along these lines ….

"I'm going to tell you a story about human nature. If we were in the US then the colleagues would probably be around the water cooler, but here in the UK it is more likely to be around a kettle, in the kitchen, making tea or coffee.

Imagine the first person says that this is a horrible place to work and they hate it here. It is human nature to avoid conflict and most people will mutter some kind of agreement, so they don't start an argument. When the third (tea-thirsty) member of staff joins the group, they ask what they are talking about. The first person says they are discussing how bad it is to work here. Gradually more and more people get drawn into the discussion.

It is extremely rare that you find someone who will say that they do not agree and that they love working here.

We cannot allow negativism on this team."

The sales manager called this story 'No Negs (negative people) on my team' because he knew that in a sales environment in particular, morale is hugely important.

MY MESSAGE IS SIMPLE

Morale has as much influence on the success of a company as the skills that the employees have. Negativism is like a cancer. It invades the organisation and spreads like a virus and must be removed as fast as possible; regardless of seniority, experience or skillset.

DELEGATION DEPENDS

Good managers delegate everything, don't they? Not necessarily.

If a manager never delegates tasks to subordinates, then they never get a chance to learn. Even worse they start to feel that they cannot be trusted with any important task. This can be hugely demoralising.

We all fall into the trap of doing the bits of our job that we like doing. If you do not, then you end up letting everyone else do the interesting stuff, and as the boss you only have the bad or difficult bits to sort out. There is clearly a dynamic tension here with no simple solution. Many business books are written by people who study business rather than do it every day. Doing something is a lot more difficult than watching or studying it. Delegation is often over-simplified.

My recommendation is this ...

Sit down with your subordinates and go through the tasks the team needs to complete. Try to delegate as many things as possible if it is clear that someone else has the skills and experience to do that task. If you find that as a manager, you still have too much to do then you need to think through who needs to be trained to take away some of your tasks. Getting junior staff to work alongside more experienced people is a great way to learn and to build teams.

What you must not do is delegate a task to someone who has never done it before and then leave them to struggle. This is the quickest way to destroy the confidence of that individual.

One of the greatest compliments I was ever given was by someone much more junior in the business. He said, "I never feel like I am working for you. I always feel like I am working WITH you."

MY MESSAGE IS SIMPLE

Delegation is a subject where one size does not fit all. However, if you do not master the art of delegation then you will drown in the volume of work and do nothing well (and your team will gradually leave).

TOO MANY PEOPLE WANTING PROMOTION AT ONCE

Some people seem to suggest that you should only recruit graduates. Surround yourself with very bright people, with lots of degrees and the business will do great. Or will it?

Life is all about balance. Too much of anything is rarely good for you.

Whenever you recruit people with degrees you need to be careful. Let's look at some real-life examples of what I have seen.

If you have seven or eight graduates in a team then they all want to get promoted regularly. How are you going to do that when you have limited opportunities for promotion? Do not be surprised if gradually some of the graduates start to leave and by the end of year two you have few left.

MY MESSAGE IS SIMPLE

The average team has seven people. You need five or six of any team to be people who are either very good at what they do but happy at that level, or junior and being trained. Not everyone wants to be the boss. This avoids there being regular rows about who should get the next promotion.

If someone does apply for a promotion and you think they are not ready, then you must give them constructive feedback. If you do not, then you can turn an opportunity for someone to get promoted, into a de-motivational exercise for everyone else.

Too many ambitious people can cause havoc.

NOW YOU ARE THROUGH THE DOOR

For many years I tried to meet (or induct) new starters within 48 hours of them joining the company. When we only had one site this was possible, but as the number of sites increased and they were geographically spread across the UK, it became impossible. Like many business owners there are some aspects of the 'early days' that I miss.

I tried to make inductions 'get to know you' meetings and I got the new starter to tell me about them and then I responded. As I was often much older, my bit sometimes took longer.

One of the things that I was keen to stress was this - whatever your background - experience or qualifications - all it did was get you through our door. From now on your promotion is entirely dependent upon how well you do, not what badges you have?

I would deliberately choose examples of how people with no previous experience and minimal educational qualifications had been promoted regularly and ended up in senior positions in the company.

Many companies operate 'fast track promotion schemes' for graduates. At the risk of being controversial; I don't believe in it.

Can you imagine how frustrating it must be if you are the star performer on your team (and often the one that other team members turn to for advice) to be told that you cannot be promoted because you do not have a degree? Even worse, someone who is recognised as not as good as you, by the rest of your team, is promoted above you? This creates huge disharmony; not only for the person incorrectly over-looked, but, also for the rest of the team. What kind of message is it sending to everyone else? There is no point trying really hard to be a great employee if you do not have the relevant educational qualifications?

Unless you are entering a profession such as accountancy, law or medicine, very few people end up having a career in their degree subject. A degree is a good indicator of someone's overall intelligence and willingness to work hard. However, they still need to earn promotions like anyone else.

MY MESSAGE IS SIMPLE

Promotion should be based on merit alone. Once you deviate from that policy your staff will remember it for a long time (and rightly so).

REMEMBERING NAMES IN LARGE ORGANISATIONS

For several years I ran Cable TV businesses. The product and service are irrelevant. These were businesses that employed well over 1,000 people. It was a bit like being a headmaster. Everyone knew my name and what I did in the company. Unfortunately, they expected me to know them as well. They had one name to remember and I had over 1,000.

This is a common problem with larger businesses. How do you tackle it?

For many years I used this technique. I do not deny that it worked incredibly well, but, eventually, was absolutely exhausting.

Let us imagine I was going to a satellite office in Essex to meet the field technicians' team.

I would arrange to meet the manager and supervisors about 15 minutes before the main meeting started. They would give me a potted overview of the staff we were about to meet and some key things about them.

I would walk into the room and immediately approach someone and say something like, "How's things? Is your son still playing hockey?" If you could remember the names of most in the room and some personal details on three-five of them then the effect was staggering. It looked like I cared about the people I was meeting, because I clearly did. Please remember that I often did this four, or five times a day, so it took a huge amount of commitment to keep this going.

Eventually, after a number of years, I realised that I was finding it harder and harder to keep up with the sheer number of new starters. When I set up my own business and I went from 1,200 people to 12, I have to admit that part of me was relieved that I could relax a little.

Later, I invented another technique that made remembering names a bit easier. Everyone in the organisation had their photographs on their email signature. It worked great with customers who felt like they knew the member of staff they were emailing (even if they had never met face-to-face). Internally it made it much easier to remember who was who?

MY MESSAGE IS SIMPLE

Technology changes, but human nature does not. We all feel special when someone remembers our name.

Most managers do not spend enough time trying to master this skill. Try having an organisation chart with photographs on it. Have a quick look at it before you enter the building or meeting room. Some tasks never seem to pay back the time invested. This is one task that will pay handsome rewards.

EMPLOYEES AND SHAREHOLDERS ARE SOMETIMES DIFFERENT

There are times when the interests of employees are exactly the same as the shareholders and other times when they are different. How do you manage this dynamic tension?

There are two types of Chief Executives (CEO's): some are employees and do not own shares, others are shareholders. I would contend that it is easier to understand and manage the interests of both employees and shareholders if the CEO owns shares. Every time an employee asks for something, they are torn about what to do?

It is human nature to consider your own interests first. An employee will be more concerned about pay and promotion prospects and a shareholder about the profitability and ultimate value of the company.

At the risk of stating the obvious: the shareholders own the company to make money. However, an enlightened shareholder understands that without committed employees a shareholder will never achieve their objectives.

If the economy is buoyant and jobs are freely available, then you often find that employers compete to offer the best packages in order to attract employees. Does that mean you can treat employees less well when the job market is not so strong? My answer is no.

You cannot over-estimate how much easier it is to work with a team who have been together for a while, and everyone knows what to do, without the constant distraction of recruiting and training. Some companies pay the lowest wage possible and argue that the job in question is totally unskilled. Again, I don't agree. If you ran, say a supermarket, but offered slightly better pay and conditions than the others, then most people would want to stay working for you. The argument against this is that if it worked then other supermarkets, in this example, would follow suit and you would simply increase costs in the labour market. Again, my answer is, try it. Others will always want to pay the lowest possible. I simply won't go there. I want the best people, who enjoy working for us, and want to stay. I think that approach has benefited shareholders the most in the long run.

MY MESSAGE IS SIMPLE

The best teams normally win, not the best individuals in a not-so-good team. Just look at Lionel Messi. He has won the Ballon d'Or for the world's best footballer six times (as at 2019) and yet he has never managed to win the World Cup with Argentina. Cristiano Ronaldo has won the Ballon d'Or five times and he has also never won the World Cup with Portugal (although he did win the Euros once).

If the only way you seem to be able to attract the best people is to pay the highest salaries, then you are doing something wrong. People should want to work for you if the pay is sensible, not necessarily because it is the best.

Sometimes this is about better conditions and not just pay, but often it is about people wanting to feel that they are valued, respected, and are doing something they can be proud of with people they like.

Shareholders like great teams; because they get the best results.

WHY THE BOSSES FACE IS IMPORTANT

I think people are now generally aware of the concept of body language and the impression it can give. As an example, someone with their arms folded can look as though they are 'closed' to an argument and not receptive to listening to someone else's point of view.

I am going to talk about a very specific piece of body language - the bosses face.

Many years ago, one of my directors took me to one side and gave me a polite dressing down. "You don't seem to understand," he said. "Your face dictates the mood of the entire organisation".

"What do you mean?" I asked.

He patiently explained that if I looked worried then the news would spread very quickly that we had serious problems. Conversely, if I was smiling and relaxed, then everyone assumed things were going well. If you think this sounds overly simplistic, as I initially did, then try it and see what happens. It is true.

MY MESSAGE IS SIMPLE

Be very careful what face you are wearing. This is even more important when you are going through a difficult spell. People want to believe that there is a plan and that the senior team are confident it will work.

However, do not take this to ridiculous extremes - you have to appear to be acting normally, even if you do have turmoil inside.

In general, people take more notice of how you behave than what you say.

THE SAME PEOPLE CAN BE GOOD, BAD AND AVERAGE

I often hear people say that we need the 'best people'. I prefer to say that we need to 'get the best out of people'.

The idea that people fit into neat categories: good, bad, and average, and never change, is way too simplistic. I will use an extreme example to illustrate the point. I will not name the business as I do not want the people involved to recognise themselves.

I took over a business that was one of 14 companies in a Group of similar companies spread across the UK. This was an industry where there were league tables on all sorts of things - financial and non-financial. On almost all league tables, my new business was bottom of the table, or quite near.

This was not a small business as it had around 1,000 employees. I wondered if they saw the situation in the same way. In a massive gamble I decided to ask every employee to attend one of two sessions in a large conference centre where I showed them all of the league tables and explained the significance of each. I told them with great passion that I didn't want to be the bottom anymore as this was my home and I felt it very personally.

The reaction was incredible.

Almost all of the 1,000 people decided that enough was enough and within an amazing year we were top, or near the top, on every league table. It was an incredible turnaround and the atmosphere was upbeat everywhere you went.

As often happens with managers: when you are perceived to have fixed a big problem, you get given another one to solve. This involved me leaving the business and joining another Group company. Early on, the new leader managed to upset quite a lot of key employees, and at the end of the next year the business was back to mid-table.

In the space of three years, the same people had been worst, best and average.

MY MESSAGE IS SIMPLE

If we are honest with ourselves; we all have good days and bad days. We perform at our best when we are interested and motivated. A group or team is simply a collection of individuals, so, do not be surprised when this happens with them as well. The same people can be good, bad and average and if you are the boss then you are possibly the reason why they are what they are at present.

YOU CAN'T SHOUT AT PLANTS

I first became a Managing Director when I was 30 years old. I quickly realised that it wasn't as much fun as I expected and in reality; it was rather stressful. Like many people of that age I had a newish house and a scruffy garden to tidy up. I'm still not a particularly good gardener but I enjoy pottering around outside. I quickly learned that 'you can't shout at plants' and make them grow faster. The best you can do, is do the right things, and then have the patience to wait.

There are some things in your work life that you can make go faster with focus but others you can't. One of the knacks in management is to spot which is which.

It also taught me that there is absolutely no role for shouting in management. I have never found any situation where shouting helps. In fact, it normally makes things worse.

MY MESSAGE IS SIMPLE

I think we all understand that children learn quicker when they are praised for good behaviour. Why do we think that we grow out of that?

IF YOU ARE THE MOST JUNIOR IN THE ROOM

One of the most frustrating things about being young and junior is that you quickly realise that you have something to say, but often don't get a chance to speak.

Here is a simple tip that might help you to get noticed. It does not always work but it is well worth trying.

If it is clear, that everyone in a meeting is thinking the same thing: then if you are the most junior person in the room, be the first to say it out loud.

It is great for your confidence when everyone else agrees with you.

MY MESSAGE IS SIMPLE

If you don't speak then you will never get heard. But, when you do speak, be brief and get straight to the point.

However, once you learn how to be brief and get straight to the point, don't lose that skill. It applies to every level in the organisation. The best leaders are the ones who can speak in simple English. Never try to make someone look foolish because they do not understand the latest buzzwords or 'management speak'. This is especially true if you work in IT or technology companies.

WHY SHADOWING IS SO POWERFUL

When I was near the end of my career as a Managing Director (MD) or Chief Executive (CEO), I couldn't fit in any more meetings. I'm not trying to sound special. It was simply that trying to run eight businesses in a Group meant that there were so many scheduled meetings that there was little space in the diary to fit in anything more. I tried something one day, and like many accidents, it turned out to be one of the best things I had done in ages.

A junior manager was curious about what happened in sales meetings. I therefore asked him to sit next to me as I spent an afternoon "talking to the wall" as a variety of sales directors, from far-flung sites, joined the webcam on the 70" TV in the Boardroom. There were five, similar but different, sales meetings. Each had a nuance about their particular vertical market or specialist products and services. In almost every meeting, someone had a very real problem that we needed to discuss. We encouraged the idea that the more brains trying to find the answer the more likely a solution would be found. The meetings were very open and often quite fun, even though serious subjects were being discussed.

At the end of each 20-minute meeting I turned to the junior manager and asked what they had learned from that session. The more the afternoon wore on, the more we talked. At the end of the five-meeting marathon I asked how he had found the experience? Rather than finding a tired-out manager, he seemed more enthusiastic than when we had begun. "I have learned more about the Group in one afternoon than I have in the last 12 months. It's not as straightforward as it looks is it?" I decided to do the exercise again, and again, and again.

For the last 18 months, or so, of my 29-year spell as MD or CEO I used to invite a different person, or sometimes team, to shadow me for the afternoon. As well as watching each meeting and then discussing what they had seen, we decided to start that afternoon by having lunch together. This gave me a chance to learn about them, and their problems, and they had an opportunity to ask me whatever they wanted. Even the business 'greats' like Steve Jobs at Apple and Larry Page at Google benefited from having Bill Campbell as a mentor.[20]

MY MESSAGE IS SIMPLE

It is easy to forget, when you attend the same meetings each week, that people who do not attend those meetings often have no real understanding of what happens. Having someone sat next to you, watching what happens, can be far more instructive for them, than you telling them what happens. At the end of the meeting you will have real-life, current, problems that you can discuss. Learning is always easier when you use real case studies. Later on, I have seen that others have tried this process and given it a fancy sounding name: flash mentoring. Try it. Showing people what happens, warts and all, is great way for them to learn. Perhaps even more importantly, I learned a huge amount from meeting new people, what their problems were, and how they would tackle the problems I faced? Sometimes their ideas were good, often not. Simply having the opportunity to explain why, their sometimes-simplistic idea, would not necessarily work, was incredibly useful to both parties. Given my time again, I would have started shadowing much earlier in my career.

---

[20] Carmine Gallo, 22 May 2019. *The 'Trillion Dollar Coach' Who Mentored Steve Jobs and the Google Guys Showed Them a Simple, Powerful Communication Tactic.* [online]. Available at <https://www.inc.com/carmine-gallo/the-trillion-dollar-coach-who-mentored-steve-jobs-google-guys-showed-them-a-simple-powerful-communication-tactic.html> Accessed on 5 March 2020

DOING PRESENTATIONS - HOME AND AWAY

One of the most stressful aspects of work is when you are asked to do a presentation. Presentations are like many things in that they get easier with practice. One of the biggest mistakes that new, often younger, people make is that they try to make their presentation impressive by showing that they understand how to use all the flashy graphics and animations.

The first time they go out to visit someone outside of their office, or home, it goes horribly wrong and there is much cursing about technology.

I sometimes used to give a presentation course called 'Presentations Home and Away'. The essence of the course was this ...

If you are in your own office environment, then you understand what facilities are available and can test that everything works. In our Boardroom, which I used every day, I knew that the best presentation format was widescreen for our TV on the wall. I knew we had fast internet access so including links to websites to do demonstrations all worked wonderfully. As soon as I left that room the world completely changed.

To illustrate this point, I once took my sales team to our lawyers in London. I asked the lawyers if we could borrow one of their meeting rooms? This was about the most corporate environment a salesperson would ever be exposed to and I was curious to see how they would perform? I simply asked them to present for 10 minutes or so, to the rest of the sales team, what they would be concentrating on for the next three months? I wanted to make the subject as easy and close to home for them as possible.

When they arrived, they asked me where the presentation screen was? I told them I didn't know, but I had only allocated the meeting an hour and they were now wasting valuable meeting time. They decided to present against a plain(ish) white wall. Not surprisingly this later ruined the resolution of the slides. Small text became illegible.

They then asked if the room had a projector? I said no. I pulled a projector out of a big bag I had taken with me.

They tried to plug the projector in and then realised that the plug sockets were on the wall, rather than under the table and the cable would not reach. To save time, I pulled an extension out of my, increasingly useful, bag.

One member of the sales team explained that he needed internet access for his presentation as he wanted to show us the websites of his key potential customers. I told him I had no idea how to access the lawyers WiFi network and he went to reception to see if an IT support person might be available to help him? It was ten minutes before an IT technician arrived. He explained that lawyers were paranoid about security, so visitors are not allowed to access their network. In addition, they had only just moved into the building and they had not yet had time to set up a guest wifi network. In short, there was no internet access for visitors.

I had allocated each of the four presenters 15 minutes. After all the messing about and waiting for the IT guy, the first presenter stood up after 40 minutes. As is often the case: they overran their 15-minute slot and spoke for 20 minutes. I then stood up and explained that my one hour meeting slot had run out and I left the room. Three of the presenters had never even got the chance to speak.

After about two minutes I returned to the room to start a discussion on the fiasco we had just witnessed.

I asked the sales team to list the different sorts of venue they might have to attend for meetings. We came up with a long list. I explained that the previous week I had travelled 300 miles to see a major customer and when I got there the manager had forgotten to book a meeting room and we had to hold the meeting in the pub next door.

At one big conference, with hundreds of wealthy investors in the audience, we asked to plug our Microsoft office laptop into the audio visual equipment only to find out that no-one had told us that the conference organisers only used Apple kit and we had two minutes to find the appropriate Microsoft-Apple adaptor lead.

One day I presented in Zurich, Switzerland. The audience managed funds worth billions of US dollars. When I plugged in my laptop, every screen with a number on it reconfigured itself into an ugly looking mess. Even worse, I was the keynote presentation, intended to end the conference on a high. Fortunately, a Swiss fund manager realised that he had a similar problem in reverse when he went to present in London. In the UK we use full stops as decimal points for numbers and commas to separate thousands. In Europe a comma is used to denote a decimal point. We hastily retyped every slide with a number on it and I stood up with seconds to spare.

Technology can throw up all sorts of problems that you have not met before. The venue of the meeting will rarely be perfect for what you want.

When we first floated on the London Stock Exchange, I was told that our company would be one of many presenting to the fund managers that day and we only had a 20-minute slot. We were therefore advised to print out our presentation and use old-fashioned handouts as we could start straight away without having to worry about finding out how the technology in the room worked. The investment managers liked it because they could hand-write notes on the side of the presentation. The next time we met them, they produced the previous presentation, with its hand-written notes.

Before you think the message is as simple as 'print out your presentation and take a hand-out with you' be careful with widescreen presentations. They look great on a widescreen TV, but somewhat ridiculous squashed onto a piece of A4 paper. I have seen people frantically trying to change their widescreen presentations to A4 format and then realised that all the graphics need completely resizing.

MY MESSAGE IS SIMPLE

You can be as clever as you want with a presentation if it is being held in a venue that you know well but be careful everywhere else.

You have been warned. Ignore this lesson at your peril.

SUCCESSFUL PEOPLE FAIL

One of the biggest differences between Americans and the British is in their attitude to failure. In Britain we still see someone who has set up a business that did not succeed as a personal failure. Why do we think that someone who has not done something before, is supposed to be good at it, when they have no previous experience?

Richard Branson is one of the most famous British businessmen ever. He has had far more failures than successes. The few successes he has had, are huge.

In times of failure, Branson has said, recognising mistakes and recovering are essential skills for an entrepreneur:

My mother drummed into me from an early age that I should not spend much time regretting the past. I try to bring that discipline to my business career.

Over the years, my team and I have not let mistakes, failures or mishaps get us down. Instead, even when a venture has failed, we try to look for opportunities, to see whether we can capitalise on another gap in the market.[21]

Here are a few of Richard Branson's businesses that failed:

1. Student Magazine
2. Virgin Cola
3. Virgin Vodka
4. Virgin Vie
5. The Virgin Cosmetics Company
6. Virgin Clothing
7. Virginware
8. Virgin Cars
9. Virgin Brides
10. Virgin Megastore
11. Virgin Pulse
12. Virgin Digital
13. Virgin Express
14. Virgin Student
15. Virgin Lottery
16. Virgin Games/Virgin Interactive

Like me, you probably cannot remember many of these Virgin brands.

There are a huge number of very talented people. Not all have been equally successful. Sometimes the difference is down to luck. Luck can make a big difference in the success of a business. If you are one of the few lucky ones

---

[21] Business Insider, 2016. *14 Virgin companies that even Richard Branson could not stop going bust.* [online]. Available at: <https://www.businessinsider.com/richard-branson-fails-virgin-companies-that-went-bust-2016-5?r=US&IR=T> [Accessed on 16 January 2019]

that are successful, please show some humility and recognise that it may not always mean that you are smarter than others.

MY MESSAGE IS SIMPLE

Trying and failing will teach you something; if you study what went wrong. It is far better to have had a go, than to have sat on the sidelines, wishing "if only".

However, enthusiasm is useless if your business plan never made sense to start off with.

CHAPTER FOUR
Operational Advice

THE POTTERS' WHEEL

I give credit for this next anecdote to our former Chairman, my great friend and mentor, Roger Wilson.

Business is like clay on a potter's wheel. If you don't regularly, pat it back into shape, it will collapse into a mess.

This is completely true. Just because one aspect of the business was going well last week, it does not mean that it will stay that way.

MY MESSAGE IS SIMPLE

Stay on top of things. It might get boring if you have to do something every day or week, but if you do not then you will soon have a mess to fix.

IF IT LOOKS TOO GOOD TO BE TRUE

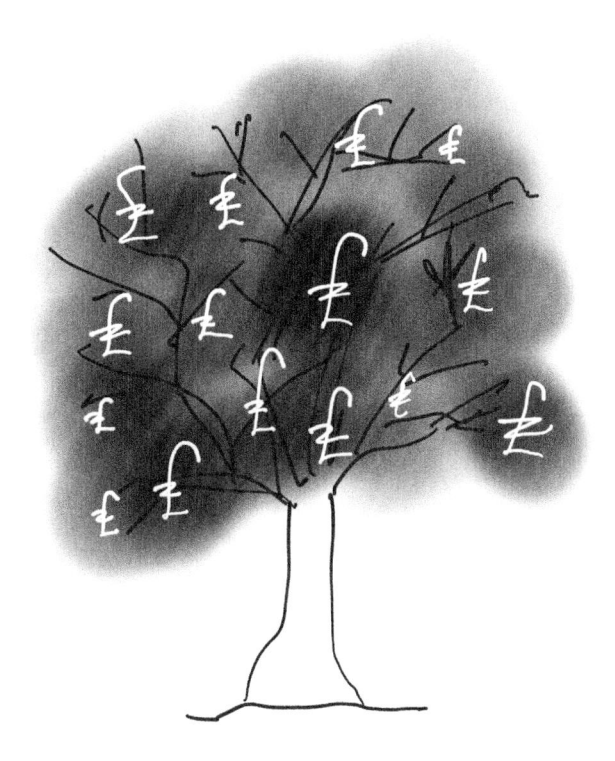

When we are under pressure, we all wish for good news. At the risk of being a killjoy, even good news should be examined a bit more closely. If the good news is incredibly good, then be wary.

There is a lot of truth in the phrase – "if it looks too good to be true – then it probably is."

MY MESSAGE IS SIMPLE

Don't just accept something simply because you want it to be true.

THE CAT AND THE BELL

What is best? A great strategy, or, a not so good strategy with great implementation? This fable illustrates my view pretty clearly.

It was 2.30pm in Mouse Town. A wild cat came charging down the High Street. It picked up a mouse, bit it's head off and threw the body against a wall. It then turned and ran off. It didn't even eat the mouse. Mouse town was stunned.

As the Town Hall clock struck 2.30pm the day after, once again the wild cat came charging down the High Street. It picked up another mouse, bit it's head off and threw the body against the wall. Again; it ran off without eating the mouse.

Not knowing what to do, the mice called a meeting (as you do when you don't know what else to do). This is horrific they all agreed, but what are we going to do? No-one knew. A little mouse pushed his way from the back of the crowd. "Let's go and see the wise old owl. He'll know what to do". They all agreed (using the well-known principle: if you don't know what to do, find someone else to delegate the problem to).

You now need to picture the following silhouette: a line of mice walking up a hill with a tall tree at the top of the hill.

The mice knocked on the tree trunk and the wise old owl looked down at them. (Don't spoil the story by suggesting, as one of my daughters did, that owls eat mice as well. This is a friendly owl; so, roll with the story).

"How can I help you?" asked the wise old owl. They explained the problem with the wild cat and the owl closed his eyes to think. Just as they thought he had gone to sleep the owl opened his eyes and said. "Put a collar with a bell on it on the cat. When you hear the bell ringing you can all run and hide before the cat gets there."

The mice skipped down the hill and then called another meeting. "Who is going to put the collar with the bell on the cat?" There were no volunteers.

The mice went back up the hill and knocked on the tree trunk again. "Oh, it is you lot again. What's the problem?" asked the wise old owl.

"Who is going to put the collar on the cat?" the mice all shouted.

The wise old owl closed his eyes again and this time they were convinced he had fallen asleep. He suddenly opened his eyes and said, "I do strategy. I don't do detail."

MY MESSAGE IS SIMPLE

A clever strategy without a detailed implementation plan is useless. Given a choice between a very clever strategy with no implementation plan and a reasonable strategy with a clear implementation plan I will always go for the latter. Business is about getting results not having an interesting chat. A strategy with no implementation plan is just a chat.

Having said that you should never forget the most famous quote from Mike Tyson, the former World Heavyweight boxing champion, "They all had a plan until I punched them in the face". All plans must be able to change quickly if things turn out to be different to what you expected.

CHURN AND THE SWITCHING PROCESS

Many of us have bought and sold a house at some point in our lives. It is a lengthy and extremely stressful process. That is why many of us, including me, vowed to not do it again for a long time.

We can learn some business lessons from the experience of moving home – people do not like moving supplier if it is extremely complex, takes ages, is very stressful and could potentially go wrong. The more products and services a customer buys from one supplier, the more complicated it is to leave.

Products and services fall into two categories: ones where it is very easy to change supplier and ones where it is not.

Let's take a look at some products and services where it is easy to change supplier and the implications of that.

Many utilities; gas, electricity or telephone lines were former monopolies. The UK Government therefore tried hard to ensure that changing supplier was a straightforward process. In many instances you simply need to fill in an online form and the process of moving to another supplier happens in days. Sometimes it does not even involve a visit to your premises. With suppliers of mobile phones, it can be even easier; as you simply have to send them a text to tell them you are changing supplier.

When it is easy to change supplier you often see huge price competition with all kinds of low headline prices. I talked in another chapter about how customers need to be wary of low headline prices as the supplier typically makes their profit in a less obvious way.

Often, in these markets, you see suppliers trying to write onerous terms and conditions so there is a financial consequence if a customer leaves them. It is an attempt to counteract the simplicity of the leaving process. Governments have often intervened to outlaw long term contracts, with high financial penalties, if you leave before the contract term is completed. Financial penalties for leaving are often restricted to an initial 12-month contract. This normally applies to consumer contracts. Note that in the EU, any business with less than 10 employees is classed as a consumer and covered by the same legislation.

MY MESSAGE IS SIMPLE

We all need to keep our customers. If the process for a customer to leave is very simple, then you need to think of ways to persuade them to stay that are not purely based on price.

Often suppliers bundle products together so that you cannot see the price of the individual items. Or, you deliberately offer cheaper pricing if you take 2 or more products. As an example: when BT entered the Sports TV market, they offered cheaper broadband to anyone taking a subscription to their Champions League Football (BT Sports) TV Channel.

The best solution is to sell lots of products and services to a customer. The more complex it is to leave, the less likely they are to do so.

However, let's add one huge caveat - you will only ever keep customers if you provide great service.

COMMON SENSE IS NOT COMMON

I think "Common Sense" is one of the most incorrectly named phrases in the English language. Unfortunately, 'common sense' isn't very common at all.

The mistake that all of us sometimes makes, is to think that because something seems to be 'common sense' to you then it must be the same to everyone else. What we decide is 'common sense' is based on our personal experiences and other people clearly have different life experiences.

You may think that putting your hand near something hot is a stupid idea and that must be common sense. We think that putting something that tastes horrible in your mouth is a stupid idea and must be common sense. A baby will only agree with you once it has had the experience of putting its' hand near something hot, or, putting something disgusting in its mouth. It must experience it before it becomes 'common sense'.

MY MESSAGE IS SIMPLE

Don't fall into the trap of thinking that common sense' is common. We all have different life experiences.

What is common sense to an engineer is probably not common sense to say a salesperson.

WHAT YOU MEASURE IS WHAT YOU GET

I sometimes get frustrated in meetings when people start to argue fervently for their point of view but have no statistics of any kind to back up their argument. In business we clearly need to measure things to see how we are doing. However, measuring things is fraught with traps. I'll give you some examples to illustrate the point.

If you tell a teenager that you will pay them £10 if they wash your car every Sunday afternoon; please don't be surprised if it happens. But also, please don't be surprised if something else, such as homework, does not get done. This is an example of 'what you measure is what you get'.

Let's look at a more detailed business example.

Many years ago, I took over a business that had serious customer service problems. There were so many customers ringing to complain that it took well over a minute to answer every call. The Group CEO gave out an ill-thought-through instruction to all Customer Service Directors that they must answer 95% of all calls within 15 seconds. So, what is wrong with that? Within four weeks our Customer Service department had hit the target.

I asked for two numbers: how many staff have you hired and how many calls are we now receiving?

To stop the Group CEO shouting at him, the Customer Service Director had hired 20 temporary workers without seeking authorisation. I didn't need a Finance meeting to tell me that our profitability had been destroyed.

The number of calls being received had gone up; not down. The temporary workers weren't trained so all they could do was take a message. No-one measured how long it took to turn a message into a resolution, or, informed the customer when a problem had been fixed. We were very slow at getting back to the customers, so, they started to ring in to check where their problem was up to. We had turned a single phone call into two or three. What a complete mess?

MY MESSAGE IS SIMPLE

What you measure is what you get. Have a long hard think about the knock-on consequences of monitoring certain things. That is why some kind of 'balanced scorecard' is often the best way forward. A single number rarely tells you everything.

WHAT SHOULD YOU MEASURE?

I talked previously about the concept of 'what you measure is what you get' and how if you measure the wrong thing then you can cause all manner of unintended consequences. The logical next question then is: what should I measure? How do I decide?

One of the common mistakes from new managers or team leaders is that they try to measure everything and give themselves so much work they are shattered and living on their nerves most of the time. Not good for the team leader and not good for anyone who works for this highly-strung individual.

Manage by exception.

Let us use an example: a faults team. If I were the Faults Team manager, I would concentrate on faults that were close to breaching their service level agreement or already have. I would assume the rest of the fault tickets are going ok and I shouldn't worry about them. We will come back later to how you check that is true.

Once you have worked out what you need to know by exception then you have to work with the IT people to ensure that these 'exceptions' are automatically flagged to you in some way. You simply do not have time to manually check everything to find which ones are the problems. As an example, an automated email may be sent to the Team Leader or manager as soon as any fault reaches one of the two categories identified earlier. If the Team Leader does not receive any emails, they can relax knowing that everything is running smoothly.

Let's go back to the faults that are supposedly going smoothly. How do you know that is true? Simply set aside a specific time each month to review a sample selection of fault calls and case histories and then give feedback to the member of staff you are checking.

MY MESSAGE IS SIMPLE

Don't be a busy fool. Manage by exception. It is quicker and more effective.

Your job is also to find the root cause of these exceptions and try to ensure they do not happen again. Repeating the same mistakes over and over again is plain stupid.

WHAT SHOULD YOU WORRY ABOUT?

At the risk of making every reader paranoid: what should you worry about (from a business perspective)?

The key to staying reasonably sane, is to reduce the list of things you worry about, as much as possible.

At the risk of making you even more paranoid - I worry about the things I do not know about rather than the things that I do. Let me explain the logic of that. If I am aware of a problem, then I will have asked someone to deal with it. As I know someone is working on the problem, I know it is on its way to probably being fixed. In contrast, if I am not aware there is a problem, then no-one is working on fixing it.

Let me give you an example to illustrate the point.

Let us imagine that one of your employees, Johnny, broke his leg unexpectedly last night and did not come into work this morning. How do you know what he was working on when he left work last night? How do you know where he was up to and which actions had been completed?

Regardless of what industry you work in, it is well worth looking at what business processes you can automate? Most jobs can be broken down into standard tasks that must be done in a specific sequence.

There are a range of software tools that you can use to automate your processes. It is well worth the time and money, setting these systems up, as they will reduce quite dramatically the number of things that you do not know about.

The beauty of business process automation is that you can log on and check what Johnny was working on last night and where he was up to? His outstanding tasks can then be reallocated to another member of staff and the work will carry on. The customers affected will probably not even be aware that the work is now being handled by a different person. Business process automation means that the number of problems we are not aware of is much reduced.

MY MESSAGE IS SIMPLE

Business process automation can be used to great effect anywhere where there is a repeatable process, regardless of industry. There is no excuse for having staff working in isolation and becoming single points of failure when something unexpectedly happens. Use the 'what would happen if he or she broke their leg unexpectedly?" test on every aspect of your business.

THERE ARE AT LEAST TWO WAYS TO ACHIEVE THE SAME RESULT

We must try to avoid thinking that our preferred way of doing something is the only way; even if it works. There is often at least two ways of achieving the same results. This applies to business and to life in general.

Let's use a life example first.

A lot of businesspeople spend years trying to earn enough money to go skiing more often. Other people, often young people, simply become skiing instructors and ski every day.

Now let's look at a business example.

I set up a business in the South East of England where salaries are very high relative to, say, the North. To ensure we were price competitive we invested heavily in business process automation and we had roughly 1/3 of the staff of many of our competitors. We bought a number of similar companies and then moved their customers to our systems so that we could create economies of scale using our automated systems.

One of our competitors was also buying similar companies to get economies of scale. They did not have the same business process automation experience that we had so they simply transferred the jobs to a region in the UK where staff costs were extremely low.

We both ended up with a similar cost structure.

This is a great example of how we both achieved roughly the same answer by two completely different approaches to the same problem.

MY MESSAGE IS SIMPLE

Try to think of the alternative ways to solve a problem and listen to others who have different ideas and approaches.

FACES NOT NUMBERS

For many years AdEPT's strapline was: 'FACES NOT NUMBERS'. It came about from a simple conversation: what do you hate about contacting a 'faceless corporation'? A faceless corporation to me is a company that does not know who you are and does not seem to treat you as anything other than a number in a queue.

We listed all the things that we hated on a flipchart and asked ourselves if there was any reason why we could not do the opposite? The answer was that there was nothing stopping us, and it did not cost money; the key was attitude and how you did things. I'll give you some simple examples ...

When a customer rings you up, give them your full name not just your Christian name. Why? I had a broadband fault one day and a guy called Dave gave me some suggestions about what to try and to ring back if it did not work: which it didn't. When I called back, I asked to speak to Dave, and was met with the response: which Dave? We have eight Dave's. If he had told me his name was Dave Foster I could have carried on the previous conversation. I now had to explain yet again the full story about my problem and how the fix had failed. The whole experience was unnecessarily frustrating.

From the day AdEPT started, all emails, letters etc have always contained a photo of the person who is sending it to you. It is remarkably effective; as customers start to believe they have physically met you when in truth they have only seen your picture.

Every time I am in the City and give out my business card with my photo on it, without fail, someone says' "That is such a simple idea I don't know why we all don't do it? Whenever I get home with a pocket full of business cards I can never remember, who is who?"

MY MESSAGE IS SIMPLE

Good customer service is a not a trendy fad that goes out of fashion. People want to be treated as individuals. That's why the full strapline is – **We are ... faces not numbers ... and so are you.**

THE 2 X 2-SEATER SOFA MEETING RULE

When I first set up my own business, I bought two 2-seater black leather sofas. They were for the restroom as we only had about 12 employees at the time.

As we had no meeting room, we used to sit on the sofas first thing in a morning. I never thought that buying two sofas would have such an incredible effect on the way we worked.

Very quickly we invented two rules:

1. If your bum didn't fit on the sofa there were too many people in the meeting, and

2. All decisions had to be made by 9.15am

As the business got larger, we had to scrap these rules, but I really missed them. The idea of restricting all meetings to no more than four people was liberating. The idea that all decisions were made by 9.15am taught us to get to the main points really quickly.

Once we had agreed what our main actions for the day were; we just got on with it. Sometimes we would be in the same room, but not have time (or inclination) to speak to each other, until tomorrow morning's meeting. The speed at which we got things done was quite astonishing.

If you want to get things done quickly; involve as few people as possible.

MY MESSAGE IS SIMPLE

Don't let people attend meetings just so they know what is going on. Everyone there, should be there, because they have a contribution to make. As your business gets bigger you will sometimes need more people in the room simply to ensure you have access to all the information you need.

Do not forget that there will be people who were not in the room who will play a vital role in what happens next. They need to understand and buy-in to the plan.

Do not fall into the trap of asking someone to type up the actions after the meeting and circulate them. Instead, display the document on a big screen everyone can see, and type the actions out as you agree them. That way everything is already done when the meeting ends, and no-one can say they weren't clear what their actions were.

STICK TO WHAT YOU ARE GOOD AT

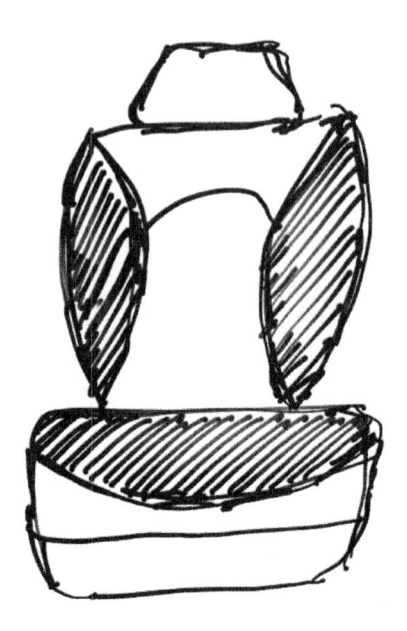

Tesla has done an incredible job raising the profile of electric cars. Early in 2019 I noticed that Tesla was worth more than Ford, despite, the fact that Ford sell millions of cars each year, and Tesla hardly any. Was this another example of investors getting carried away with a sexy story? I decided to have a more detailed look.

The share price of Tesla peaked in mid-2017 and had dropped about 28% by the end of 2018. Great if you invested early on, but you have lost a fortune if you invested in 2018. So, what is the problem?

In 2016 Tesla announced the launch of Model 3 the "first electric car for the masses". Over 400,000 people paid a $1,000 deposit based on a promise that they would be making 5,000 Model 3 cars a week by the end of 2017. Part way through 2017, the target for December 2017, was reduced to 2,500 cars a week. At the end of March 2018 Tesla announced that they had made 2,000 cars in a week for the first time. I have talked before about how it always takes longer than you think to launch a new product. Tesla will not confirm the exact reason for the delays but if the strong rumours are true then it is yet another enlightening case study.

In 2017, Reuters reported that "the strong rumour is that Elon Musk got so fed up with the poor quality of the car seats that Tesla decided to make them themselves". [22] If an experienced car seat manufacturer was finding it hard to manufacture the exacting design, why are we surprised to hear that someone who has never made car seats before, has found it extremely difficult to make them, in large quantities, very fast? The rumours are that the production line has been waiting for car seats. What a ridiculous situation to get yourself into, (if it is true)?

Why does it matter? Tesla has little income at present as it isn't selling many cars. If this carries on for much longer, they may run out of cash and may need to borrow billions of dollars (again).

MY MESSAGE IS SIMPLE

Stick to what you are good at and outsource the rest to specialists.

---

[22] Alexandria Sage, 2017. REUTERS Technology News. *Tesla's seat strategy goes against the grain ... for now.* [online]. Available at <https://www.reuters.com/article/us-tesla-seats-idUSKBN1CV0DS>. [Accessed on 18 January 2020]

THE HOW-TO-END-A-MEETING RULE

Some meetings are effective, but many are a complete waste of time. Here are some tips for making a meeting more effective ...

Invite as few people as possible; only the ones you really need.

Most meetings fall into one of two categories: **information sharing** or **decision making.**

MY MESSAGE IS SIMPLE

Make sure you are clear which of these two the meeting is meant to be. If this is meant to be a decision-making meeting, then at the end ask everyone this:

Can I summarise what I think I have heard?

This will show people you have been listening and if you have mis-understood something (which I often do) then someone will correct you before you leave the room.

Ask "what is stopping us making a decision now?"

If you need more information, then ensure someone has a clear action to get the information you need and to share it within a specific timescale. Otherwise take the decision there and then as there is no reason to prevaricate and put it off. You will simply end up getting back together again and going over the same points again (yawn, bored already).

The only exception to this rule is where the consequences are huge.

If you have all the information you need then go home and sleep on it before deciding – but only for one day not a week.

GIVE THE WOMAN A CHICKEN

One day I went to visit a supermarket in America that had the highest sales per square foot in the world. This was incredible given that it was family owned and only had two supermarkets. A small business had beaten the giants like Walmart and Tesco, so I went to have a look to understand why?

The owner was incredibly innovative. Many of his ideas have been copied and are now commonplace, but everything has to start somewhere. He realised that if customers could smell food, they were more likely to buy it. He was the first to introduce in-store bakeries and rotisserie chicken counters.

While I was there a woman walked up to the rotisserie counter and plonked a package wrapped up in silver foil on the counter. She opened it and there was the carcass of a chicken in the foil.

"The chicken was horrible," she said. "It was burned on one side and was really dry. I want my money back."

The man behind the counter looked at her disbelievingly. "Don't be ridiculous," he said. "You've eaten the chicken. That is just a bag of bones. I can't refund you for a chicken you have already eaten."

"I have four teenage sons," she said. "If anything stands still for more than 30-seconds they'll eat it. What do you expect me to do? Tell them that I have thrown away Sunday lunch and they have nothing to eat?"

"I'm not refunding the money" said the rotisserie manager.

She was now furious and shouted things at the top of her voice that I won't write down. The whole supermarket turned to stare. She finished by shouting as she stormed through the exit door, "I'll never shop here again."

The owner went over to the rotisserie manager and said, "The average customer in our supermarket spends £100 per week. (Ok, I have changed the currency to pounds rather than dollars). That is about £5,000 per year. That lady looked about 35, so over the next 30 years she would probably have spent around £150,000 with us. There are only two supermarkets in this small town and now she will probably spend it with the supermarket down the road. Give the woman a chicken."

MY MESSAGE IS SIMPLE

There will always be 'ups and downs' in a long-term relationship. Always keep an eye on the potential lifetime value of a customer. Sometimes you have to give little things away.

PS – a funny true story

The 'Give the Woman a Chicken' story was one of a series of stories I used to tell in a 60-minute talk called 'A walk across America'. When I was in Cable TV I had well over a thousand staff and we regularly hired local theatres so that we could talk to 2-300 staff at a time. One year we decided I should talk about examples of best customer service in different industries. I used to wander on to the stage with a shopping bag. I would pull an item out of the shopping bag and it reminded me to tell a story about that object. Each day the objects came out of the bag in a random order. This meant that the presentation was always slightly spontaneous.

The only consistent bit was that I always left the 'Give the Woman a Chicken' story until the end. I would pull a rubber chicken out of the bag and then throw it into the audience and shout "catch". The 'chicken' story became quite well remembered, partly for this reason.

On the final day of the tour the organisers forgot to tell me that we had run out of rubber chickens. As I stooped to pull the final item out of the bag, I found a chicken in a tray with a plastic wrapper on it. Trying not to look phased by this I picked up the chicken and threw it into the audience as normal.

I had been speaking to 300 people for nearly an hour and the adrenalin was pumping. I had missed the most important bit: the chicken was frozen. I had launched a potentially lethal object into the audience.

One of the service technicians had heard the talk before and had come back to listen to it again. He immediately realised my mistake. He was a mad keen amateur rugby player and jumped into the air as though this was a practice line-out. He caught the frozen chicken in the air. The audience thought this was the planned end of the act and burst into spontaneous applause. He theatrically bowed to the audience and smiled at me.

I have long since forgotten his name, but he saved me from one of those infamous tabloid headlines – "Boss kills employee with frozen chicken".

None of us are perfect.

FACTS VERSUS EMOTIONS: STAFFING MODELS

When people get stressed, meetings can run the risk of getting a bit emotional. At the risk of sounding like a robot, I am not a great fan of taking decisions purely based on emotions.

One of the most common discussions that can get emotional is one about staffing levels. If a team leader or manager is under pressure, then the easy way out is to blame lack of staff. If a high-profile customer has had a significant problem and they have escalated the issue, then 'lack of staff' can often be a convenient way of ensuring that the blame is someone else's fault.

In most operational departments there is a fairly scientific way of working out whether you have the right staffing numbers or not. I always insisted that my departments that employed the most people eg call centres, had a detailed staffing model to calculate how many people they need. What do I mean by that?

If a staffing model does not exist, then it is an incredibly useful way of getting a manager to understand their own department better. Let's use a call centre as an example, although the principles are the same for all operational functions.

Get them to start by analysing how many incoming contacts (calls, emails, letters etc) they are receiving every month and to check whether there are any peaks and troughs. As a simple example: it is highly predictable that the number of people ringing in to pay a bill always occurs several days after the customers receive their monthly bills. Do not forget to check whether the contacts/activity peak at certain times in the day?

Stage 2 is to analyse these incoming contacts into categories eg how many are fault calls, orders for new products, queries about delivery times etc. If you analyse several months data, you will almost certainly find a pattern and the top 6 or so types of contacts normally constitute over 90% of the workload. We are now starting to see the wood for the trees.

Review the top 6 contact types in detail to understand how long it typically takes to complete that task to the customers satisfaction. Once you realise how long it takes to do something, then you can ask yourself whether the amount of time being taken is too long; because the process isn't very efficient. Do not fall into the trap of simply hiring more people just because the process is inefficient. Fix the process and then decide how many people you need.

You then need to work out what you can reasonably expect from one employee. Start with the hours worked and then start to knock off unproductive time. What is the average level of sickness? How many holidays do staff have, and when in the year, do they normally take them? How long are lunch and coffee breaks? Remove any training courses and regular feedback meetings with management. The number of 'available' hours will often be much less than you initially thought. Do not fall into the trap of thinking that people can work flat out at 100% productivity for 100% of the available time. They need some time to recuperate in the day. Make sure that you recognise that new starters will not be as productive as experienced staff but will get better over time.

MY MESSAGE IS SIMPLE

Creating a staffing model will help you to understand how your department works. You are more likely to win requests for more staff, if you can show empirically, why current volumes of activity require it. At the end of every month you should calculate the previous months volumes by category and put them into your staffing model. It will show you how much slack you have or whether your department is starting to struggle with the volume of work. This is not a one-off exercise. It should become part of your monthly routine. Believe me - taking the emotion out of meetings where you are requesting increased staffing levels will make your work life much less stressful.

CHAPTER FIVE
Product Development

SIX WEEKS FROM LAUNCH

The most dangerous sentence in product development is "we are about six weeks from launch'".

Once I hear someone say that then I know they are so wedded to this product that they will see it through to the bitter end. It never takes six weeks. There will always be last minute technical problems and support system issues. Next we'll realise that customers have never heard of our new product and there is no stampede to buy it. By the time we have installed enough product and got enough revenue/margin to even pay the cost of the product teams wages it is normally 18 months.

The most common reason for new product companies going bankrupt is because they don't understand that 'Six weeks from launch' is 18 months from making any money. They normally haven't raised enough money to pay the wages during that period and go bust.

My businesses were different: we had older products that are very profitable and generate loads of cash to pay the wages of the new product teams.

MY MESSAGE IS SIMPLE

Every morning the new product team should go to the older product team and thank them for paying their wages and giving them the luxury of time to fix their problems.

HOW TO CHOOSE A SUPPLIER?

When I choose a supplier, I am looking for stability. Stability in a supplier comes in two categories: technical stability and financial stability.

Let's take a look at technical stability first.

When a new product is launched it often doesn't work consistently. The fault rate is high and there are lots of teething problems to sort out. If you launch a product too soon, when the product is not yet technically stable, there is a danger that you are using your customers as guinea pigs. I doubt many salespeople are entirely honest and tell the customer that the product may not work. Or at least not work consistently, or, in all scenarios.

My view on technical problems is that eventually some clever person will find a solution and then the product will work exactly as it was intended to. You simply need to keep an eye on where a product is up to, and don't be tempted to launch it too early.

Fixing financial stability is much more difficult. Let me give you an example.

We were considering launching a new product based on supplying phone calls over broadband connections. The technical guys called it VoIP (Voice over Internet Protocol). We identified 35 suppliers of this newish technology. I asked for a credit check on all 35 companies. It showed that many were new startups and all 35 were losing huge amounts of money. When we looked more closely at how they were surviving, when they were losing so much money, it became clear that the owners were regularly writing cheques for between £500,000 and £1,000,000. You have to be extremely wealthy to keep writing cheques of that size.

As we predicted, many of the early entrants into the market under-estimated how long it would take to fix the technical problems and to start earning revenue. Many, sadly, went bankrupt and the brave owners lost all their investment.

MY MESSAGE IS SIMPLE

Do not sell a customer a product or service on say, a 3-year contract, if you are not convinced that your supplier will survive the three years. Your customers will, quite rightly, not forgive you. They are not guinea pigs.

LEADING EDGE OR BLEEDING EDGE?

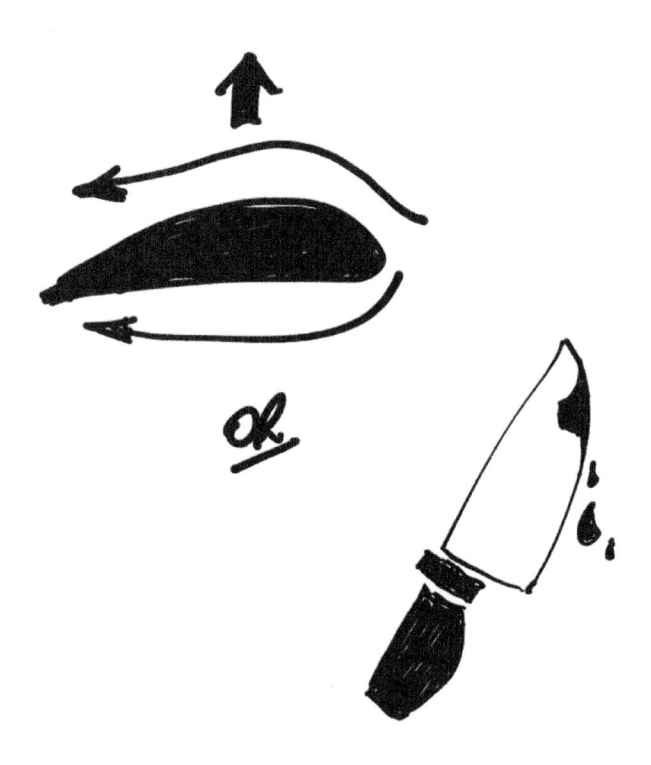

I have been involved in developing a lot of products in my career. It takes you a while to realise that there are essentially two types of development scenarios:

1. Leading edge, and
2. Bleeding edge

The one to avoid is 'bleeding edge' technology. What do I mean by that? There are some products that are so new and innovative that they are incredibly exciting but cause an unbelievable number of problems. I call these 'bleeding edge' products. Let me give you an example.

In the 1990s the UK was the only country in the world that deregulated so far that one company would be allowed to sell cable TV, telecoms and internet. All of these technologies were new to the general public and that is why it was so exciting. However, it wasn't as simple as working out how the technology worked (at scale) and raising the money to fund it.

Every aspect of the support operation was new. You couldn't buy a billing system because no-one had ever sold these products together before; so, you had to write one yourself. You couldn't buy a customer management system as no-one had ever done this before; so, you had to write one yourself. Are you getting the picture? Every aspect of our business was a trail blazer. So, the number of things we had to develop ourselves, seemed to grow every week. Before we had developed the solution to last months' problems; we seemed to find a new set of problems we hadn't thought of.

Sometimes, the amount of change you are trying to do, all at once, is simply too much for an organisation to handle. This is what I call 'bleeding edge'.

Leading edge is when you are trying to launch a product that is either 2nd to market or where you are doing something where you can use some standard systems or technologies to help you. In other words, not everything is new.

I am a great fan of being a fast second mover. It is very difficult to tell in advance which of the early products in a new market will become the market leader. If you watch a new market for a while, before entering, you are more likely to work with the winner.

One of the most famous examples to learn from is the story of video cassette recorders in the 1970s and 1980s.

Customers loved the idea of watching films or TV programmes on a video they could keep and watch when they wanted. There were two competing technologies: VHS (from JVC) and Betamax (from Sony). In many respects Betamax had superior picture technology.

However, the early Betamax tapes were only 60 minutes long and you could not record a full movie. VHS launched tapes that were initially two and later four hours long. JVC realised that movies were the key to success and did deals with the major motion picture companies. By 1987 the Video Cassette Recorder market was worth $5.25 billion in the US alone and was based on the VHS format.

If you had decided to build a business on selling Betamax players, you would have gone bust along with the product. Even though Betamax had the best picture quality it did not matter. What mattered was what the consumers wanted: to record and watch movies.[23]

---

[23] Analog: A legacyboxblog. *The tale of the tapes: how VHS ultimately beat out*

Let's take a look at another story, that is about an even more famous company who came to the market second. MySpace was launched well before Facebook and was aimed at the same audience. MySpace sold for a huge amount of money to Rupert Murdoch's News Corporation. You would have thought that a great idea, first mover advantage and the backing of a hugely successful, well-funded company would have guaranteed success. But, it didn't. When Facebook launched it continually changed itself to follow what its customers and users wanted. The growth of Facebook was spectacular. In 2010 MySpace lost $350million and faced closure.[24]

The other advantage of being a fast second mover is that it is not always clear whether there is a market for a product, no matter how smart it seems. Does the market really want that particular product and are people prepared to pay that price? Sitting and watching for a while might not be as exciting as being first mover, but it is often a much better way of making money.

MY MESSAGE IS SIMPLE

Just like you should not get seduced by selling the glamorous products (rather than the ones that make money), you should be careful of trying to be a 'bleeding edge' pioneer if you do not have the size and funding to withstand the inevitable delays and cost over-runs that come with being first to market.

I can already hear you saying that if everyone adopted that philosophy, we would never have had Facebook etc etc. Very true: but there are far more product development failures than the handful of very famous successes.

Betamax [online]. Available at: <https://legacybox.com/blogs/analog/vhs-beat-betamax> [Accessed on 31 January 2020]
[24] Adam Hartung, 14 Jan 2011. *How Facebook beat MySpace*. [Online]. Available at <https://www.forbes.com/sites/adamhartung/2011/01/14/why-facebook-beat-myspace/#b8fec7e147e9> [Accessed on 27 Feb 2020]

INNOVATION IS ...

When people talk about innovative products, they often refer to some clever technology or new idea. I think imaginative technical ideas are only one aspect of innovation. The other aspect is commercial innovation.

Let me give you a few examples:

ROLLS ROYCE

In 2012 Rolls Royce, the world's 2nd largest supplier of aircraft engines, celebrated the 50th anniversary of their 'Power-by-the-Hour' programme. In 1962 they realised that buying an engine for an aircraft was expensive and if it didn't work, for whatever reason, then that plane could not earn any money.

They decided to stop selling engines and instead started to lease them. The clever part was that the customer only paid for each hour the aircraft was flying. By sharing the risk with their customers, they showed their confidence in their product.[25]

VERY

Very.co.uk is a successful website selling clothes, homewares etc. When you buy anything you automatically qualify for their TAKE 3 policy:

"Spread the cost of any new purchase into 3. Make 3 payments, over 3 months, and pay no interest."[26]

The idea of spreading a payment over three months with no interest is very popular. The products are probably not the cheapest and therefore you are effectively paying the interest charge in the purchase price, but it does not feel that way. If you fail to pay on time, then you are charged, a whopping 39.9% interest.

GOOGLE EDUCATION PRODUCTS

I asked a very senior buyer in the UK education sector whether Microsoft or Google was likely to end up as the largest supplier of education software? Their instantaneous answer was Google. I was curious as to why? It is so much easier to buy the Google products. They have been designed specifically for Education and you can buy them and start using them in minutes by simply logging on. The perception of Microsoft is that they are trying to sell commercial products to education buyers eg Office 365, in the same way as they normally do in the commercial market, with complex licenses.

CLOUD-HOSTED PRODUCTS

Let's start by explaining what I mean by 'Cloud-hosted products.'
Traditionally most businesses had computer servers on-site. Increasingly these servers are hosted at a data centre somewhere off-site. This is often referred to as cloud-computing.

---

[25] Rolls Royce, 2012. *Rolls Royce celebrates 50th anniversary of Power-by-the-Hour.* [online]. Available at <https://www.rolls-royce.com/media/press-releases-archive/yr-2012/121030-the-hour.aspx> Accessed on 3 March 2020

[26] Very, 2020. *Take 3. 3 payments, 3 months, pay no interest.* [online]. Available at <https://www.very.co.uk/web/en/take3.page> Accessed on 4 Mar 2020

The common perception is that there is no capital expenditure with hosted products you simply rent the product each month. This is a commercial pricing decision. It is not an inherent part of the technology. You can charge for hosted products however you wish.

UBER and AIRBNB

Both Uber and Airbnb have completely disrupted their industries; taxis and hotels. Both have used clever apps and smart technology, but they have also used a different commercial approach to the previous industry norm.

When you set up an Uber account you enter your bank card details. You never need to do it again (until your card expires). As a parent I take great comfort from the fact that our daughters can always get home after a night out; even if they have no money or have lost their purse. Uber has made it easy to buy their services.

Airbnb has made it easy for homeowners to rent out their spare rooms.

MY MESSAGE IS SIMPLE

Think innovatively from a commercial perspective. Try to be your industries disruptor. You don't want to be a Blockbuster that eventually died because it never changed its business model renting VHS videos.

CHAPTER SIX
Capital Expenditure

WHAT IS CAPITAL EXPENDITURE?

Let's start by ensuring we all understand what Capital Expenditure is ... this is the Wikipedia definition

Capital expenditure or capital expense (capex or CAPEX) is

the money a company spends to buy, maintain, or improve its fixed assets, such as buildings, vehicles, equipment, or land. It is considered a capital expenditure when the asset is newly purchased or when money is used towards extending the useful life of an existing asset, such as repairing the roof.

Capital expenditures contrast with operating expenditure (opex), which are ongoing expenses that are inherent to the operation of the asset. Opex includes items like electricity or cleaning.

The dividing line for items like these is that the expense is considered capex if the financial benefit of the expenditure extends beyond the current fiscal year. [27]

MY MESSAGE IS SIMPLE

The key point is that last sentence - Capex is something that has a benefit beyond this financial year.

Do not fall into the trap of thinking that Capex is boring because constant over-spending on Capex is often what ruins companies.

Let's look at some examples in the next stories.

---

[27] Wikipedia, 2020. *Capital Expenditure.* [online]. Available at: <https://en.wikipedia.org/wiki/Capital_expenditure> [Accessed on 16 January 2020]

THE ONLY THING I'VE LEARNED ABOUT PUBS AND RESTAURANTS

In the UK, there were some large breweries, owned by famous families. I won't name who this is, but I listened to one of the family members who was in his early 70's.

He played down his understanding of the business by saying, "The only thing I have learned about pubs and restaurants is that if we refurbish them every three years we lose loads of money and if we refurbish them every seven years, or longer, then we have a chance of making money."

He clearly understood a lot about the pub and restaurant sector but had managed to boil down the business plan into one key issue. Let's have a look at what he meant. Let us assume that it costs £500,000 to refurbish a pub or restaurant and it makes £100,000 a year in profit.

If you refurbish it every three years, then you spend £500,000 and only recoup £300,000 (3 years at £100,000) so you lose £200,000 every three years.

If you refurbish it every seven years, then you spend £500,000 and recoup £700,000 (7 years at £100,000) so you make £200,000 every seven years.

The pub and restaurant businesses are clearly more complicated than this, but the lesson applies to many sectors: if you have to constantly re-invest capital expenditure in the business then there is a real risk that you will never make any money.

MY MESSAGE IS SIMPLE

We started this book by talking about cash, and we always eventually come back to cash. If you have to keep injecting lots of money into your business each year, because the profits just don't seem enough to put cash in the bank, then you need to rethink how you are doing things or do something else. Businesses that have huge, regular, capital expenditure costs, more often than not end up badly.

NOT ALL CAPITAL EXPENDITURE IS EQUAL

When we looked at the definition of Capital Expenditure, I pointed out that the key issue was this: it is about buying an asset that will have a useful life longer than the current financial year. Does that mean that all Capital Expenditure is similar? I don't think so.

Let's have a look at a few examples.

If you buy a car you know what you are getting and what the cost is. You can also set a policy about how often you buy a new one: let's say every three years. The car does not come with any financial promises attached to it. It is often what I call a 'hygiene factor' - you have to have one to do your job.

If you spend money developing a piece of software hoping you can sell it, then we have a completely different set of circumstances. Do I know exactly what I am getting for my money? You can only answer yes if there is a crystal-clear specification of what that software will do. This is often not the case. The specification can change throughout the development as people come up with new ideas. Some of these ideas will be better ways of doing what you set out to do and other ideas will expand the original idea: what is often referred to a 'project creep'.

Do you know what the exact cost of the software will be? The answer is normally no. The forecast cost when you start out can only ever be an educated guess. It will always be wrong to a greater or lesser extent.

The car had a clear useful life: three years. How long software will last may depend upon your competitors and whether they come up with something better?

When you spend capital expenditure to develop a new product you also need to guess the sales income and how much margin you will make? Inevitably, like all guesses, it will be wrong.

It is rare that a new product is finished and then you never need to spend any more money updating it. The original cost forecast has an uncanny habit of always going up.

MY MESSAGE IS SIMPLE

The whole idea of Capital Expenditure is that if you spend some money now then you might do better over the next few years. Unfortunately, the future is not guaranteed.

Be very wary of committing yourself to huge projects where you are not clear how much it is going to cost. If in doubt be conservative and live to fight another day. The world is littered with brave fools who 'bet the ranch' on a supposedly good idea.

If you do have to start a project where the costs (and potential revenues) are unclear, then break it into small phases and decide whether you want to move to the next phase each time. It is difficult, but wise, to walk away from a product and accept it is not going to succeed, rather than throw good money after bad. Americans call it 'sunk costs.'

THE DIFFERENCE BETWEEN SIMPLE AND COMPLEX CAPEX

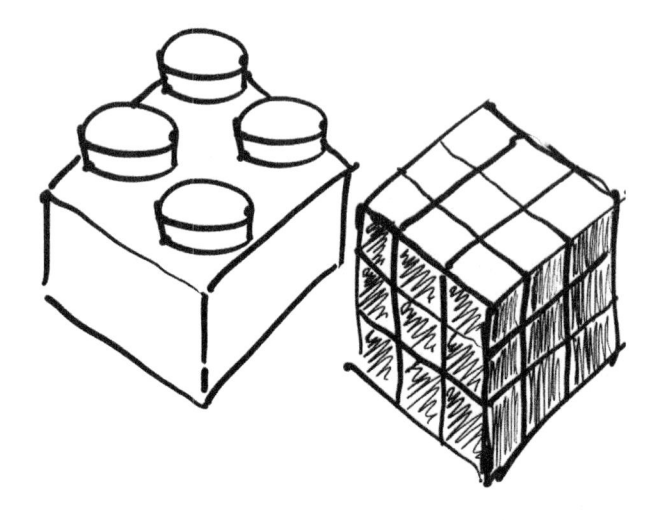

In the last story we looked at buying items such as company cars. I call this sort of item 'SIMPLE CAPEX'. You know exactly what you are getting and what it will cost. The key issue here is how much you spend each year on 'Simple Capex'?

Is it true that you only have to spend some money every three years eg when you need a new car? Or, is there regularly something to buy, and the total spend seems to be very similar each year? I have lost count of the times a business owner has said to me that last year was particularly heavy on Capital Expenditure; because we had to buy X, Y and Z. However, when you look at the accounts, the year before they had to buy A, B and C, and the year before D, E and F, and the costs do not vary much each year. If the 'Simple Capex' spend is similar every year then you might as well treat this as a cost of doing business.

I don't necessarily have a problem with regular simple Capital Expenditure. Let's invent an example ... if every year you need to spend £100,000 on various capital items just to keep going, but the business makes £1,000,000 profit a year then you can clearly afford it.

Businesses are often valued on a multiple of their profit. I think this is wrong. If there is a fairly consistent spend each year on Capital expenditure, then a better measure is a multiple of profit less Capital Expenditure. There is a big difference between a business that makes £1 million profit and only has £100k Capital expenditure and another business that makes £1 million profit, but regularly spends £600k on Capital Expenditure. In the first instance the business generates £900k cashflow a year. The second only generates £400k.

'Complex' capital expenditure needs a lot more thinking about. When the Capital Expenditure is so large and complex that it costs more than one years' profit, and sometimes takes more than one year to complete, then there is clearly a risk that you might not get your money back. I used to approve the 'simple capital expenditure' first, so that I could understand how much that cost in total and more importantly how much money we had left to use on 'complex capital expenditure'?

If a complex project costs more than one year's profitability then you need to do a cashflow forecast for the next three years (at least) to understand whether you have sufficient cash to pay for the project or whether you need to raise some money by borrowing or issuing new equity? You will be in a much stronger negotiating position if you approach a bank at the start of a project, than if you go to them part way through a project, when you are running out of cash.

MY MESSAGE IS SIMPLE

Before you embark on 'complex' capital expenditure projects make sure that you understand the various tax incentives or grants that might help you reduce the overall cost. Talk to your tax accountant. They prepare business tax claims every day and will be up to date with the latest schemes and incentives. It upsets me to see so many small businesses not claiming the tax benefits to which they are entitled. Never forget the original message in the book: businesses go bust when they run out of cash. Buying a car or van is simple. Developing software or building a new factory is not. All capital expenditure is not equal: split it between 'simple' and 'complex'. In the next section we'll look in more detail at how to review 'complex' capital expenditure.

EVALUATING COMPLEX CAPEX - FUNCTIONALITY OR VOLUME?

Each year, as part of the budget process, someone would bring me a list of items they would like to spend Capital Expenditure (CAPEX) money on in the next year. I would ask them to allocate each item to a category. I wanted to understand: why we were doing it? And perhaps more importantly: whether we had a choice?

We talked earlier about 'SIMPLE CAPEX'. This can be classified as a simple cost of doing business eg buying cars, mobile phones, laptops etc. Even in this category there might be occasional larger items eg new computer servers.

'COMPLEX CAPEX" should be broken into two categories: Volume-related' and 'New Functionality' Let's discuss the easy one, first: volume-related capital expenditure.

Let's imagine we are supplying highly secure garaging facilities for expensive classic cars. A salesman arrives and announces that he has won a contract for us to garage another ten classic cars. The question is straightforward - do we have enough space in the existing garage to accommodate these cars or do we have to set up another garage? This is what I call 'success-based CAPEX'. Even in this example, we still have to check whether we already have spare capacity before rushing off and buying something new.

Let's do another example. We run a farm growing wheat. We win a contract to supply a big bakery, so we need more fields growing wheat. We already have one combine harvester. The question again is one about spare capacity - can the existing combine harvester cover all of the fields or do we need to get another one? This leads to another question: do we have to buy one or should we rent it? Is the new contract profitable enough to pay for the extra CAPEX? Often salespeople sell products regardless of whether we have spare capacity left. Their commission schemes often don't care if a sale forces the business to buy extra capacity of something.

The 'Functionality' category needs a more detailed review and debate. Why do we need to offer customers increased functionality? Are they prepared to pay for it and in what volume? How long will it take for us to recoup our money?

Let's continue with the farm example. A salesperson wins a contract to supply fruit. The manager wants to buy a robotic fruit picking machine. This is completely new functionality to us. Does it make sense to buy a robotic fruit picker? At what volume does it become cheaper to use a robot than a human? How long is the contract we have won? If it is only a one-year contract, to see how we perform, then are we really going to spend lots of money on the hope it is renewed? How many years will it take to get our money back?

MY MESSAGE IS SIMPLE

So long as you review existing spare capacity, you do not need to worry about the volume related Capital Expenditure as you will only need to buy that item if your sales team have been successful.

When trying to decide whether to go ahead with 'functionality' improvements then a good measure of the risk is how long it takes to recoup your money? The longer it takes; the more likely it is that the forecast will be wrong.

CHAPTER SEVEN
Some Quick Maths Tricks

HOW TO MAKE MATHS YOUR FRIEND

Some people seem naturally good at mathematics; just as others are good at athletics. But, a lot of people are not great at maths. Do not let this stop you! Many entrepreneurs who have a great idea just get on with it.

Yes, business involves numbers, but you should not be afraid of maths. In business you do not need to be great at maths: you just need to be able to tell the difference between what is important and what is not?

In business you are there to make money. That means that big numbers are more important than small ones. That seems a really obvious statement, but I can't count the number of times I have found someone working really hard on a problem that costs next to nothing.

MY MESSAGE IS SIMPLE

Do not try to be the master of everything. Few successful businesspeople are good at every aspect of business. Surround yourself with people who are good at the bits you cannot do or do not like doing.

In the next few sections we'll look at a few 'maths tricks' that might make your life a bit easier.

WHY THE TIN-OF-BEANS RULE SAVES TIME

Most people can understand and remember pictures far better than complex mathematics. I grew up near the Heinz factory that makes the baked beans we all love. We can all picture a tin of beans and we know they don't cost very much.

Whenever someone brings me an issue that is not worth a lot of money I simply say, "Why are you bothering me with a tin of beans?"

Very quickly I can hear senior managers saying, "Don't bother him with that he'll just say it's a tin of beans".

MY MESSAGE IS SIMPLE

We are all incredibly busy, so, spend time on big stuff. Don't waste your working life on something that is a 'tin of beans'.

You get results by solving three big financial problems, not three little ones. Or put another way - don't be a busy fool.

HOW DO YOU SPOT A SPREADSHEET YOU SHOULD NOT TRUST?

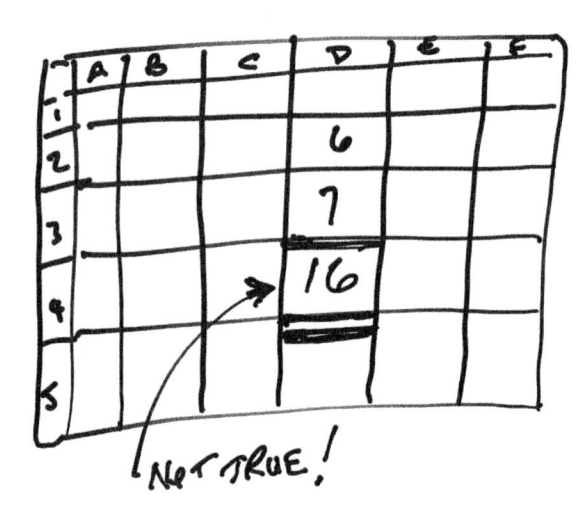

Business is full of spreadsheets and it is easy to fall into the trap of believing everything that you see on a spreadsheet (especially if you are not confident with numbers).

How do you easily spot a spreadsheet that you potentially should not trust?

TIP 1

Look at a column with numbers in it. If the numbers are centred and some have one decimal point, others two decimal points and others three decimal points it tells you immediately that the person who did the spreadsheet, does not understand Excel very well, as formatting is relatively straightforward.

Experienced people right align numbers with commas for thousands and the same number of decimal points on every row. Why? So that you can easily see which are the large numbers!

TIP 2

Look for a cell that should be a calculation such as a total. Click on the cell. If the number is typed in (rather than a calculation), it immediately tells you that the person does not know how to do even the most basic calculations using Excel and has calculated the number on an old-fashioned calculator and then typed the number in. This is fraught with all sorts of fat finger errors.

MY MESSAGE IS SIMPLE

A spreadsheet in the hands of an inexperienced person is extremely dangerous. If you need Excel training; please tell your boss. Don't pretend you know what you are doing. You will get found out when the xxxx hits the fan.

This next generalisation might cause howls of protest ... a lot of salespeople are great at talking and selling but are not necessarily good at spreadsheets. However, salespeople often need to use spreadsheets to do quotations for customers. When you first hire a new salesperson, ask them to take you through one of their spreadsheet quotes. You can always tell them that you are trying to understand how much money you make on selling those particular products ie any excuse to take a look. Do it early in their career with you. That way you very rapidly understand which salespeople you can trust on their own and which need spreadsheet assistance or training.

WHEN 'NEARLY' IS GOOD ENOUGH

Quick! Run! There's loads of them!

There is a danger that we always think we need to be precise and exact. In business it just isn't true. Often getting the number and sentiment nearly right is good enough. We are going to look at the power of rounding.

Let's say someone sells 19 items at £21 each. To work out the total revenue we need to multiply 21x19. This is a complicated calculation. If we round both numbers to the nearest 10 then we are multiplying 20x20 = 400. This is a much easier calculation.

The correct answer of 19x21 is 399. By rounding the numbers, we got it nearly right. I think that is close enough to have a rough idea of the number. The accountants need the exact numbers for their job, but as a manager we are normally using numbers as an aid to take decisions. We just need the number to be close enough to help.

You may have noticed in that example that we rounded one number upwards (19 to 20) and one down (21 to 20). That means the rounding nearly cancelled each other out.

Let's look at another example where we only round up one of the numbers. 18x19 = 342. If we round up the 19 to 20 then 18x20 (a much easier calculation) = 360 ... as we have only rounded up, we know our rounded guess is too high. If we say the answer is "a bit less than 360" - does it matter the actual answer is 342? We know roughly what the answer is?

The key question is this - would we take a different decision if the answer was 342 rather than 360? If the answer is no, then why are we worried about the exact number? We are trying to take a decision, not fill in a tax return.

The idea that, 'nearly is good enough' does not just apply to numbers. Meg Whitman is the only female (I can think of) to have lead two of the giant US Corporations: eBay and HP. In her 2010 book, "The Power of Many: Values for Success in Business and in Life," she summarised this in one sentence: "Perfect" is the enemy of 'good enough.' [28]

There are few things in business that need perfection. We are not all hand-making Swiss watches. Inaction is the problem. Waiting for a perfect solution can mean that nothing gets done. Sheryl Sandberg, COO of Facebook, in her book "Lean In: Women, Work, and the Will to Lead" put it another way, "Done is better than perfect."[29]

MY MESSAGE IS SIMPLE

Once you get used to using rounded numbers, rather than trying to do complex calculations, we can now use two great techniques together. Before you ask a question, guess the answer, but if you have to do it quickly guess the answer using rounded numbers. I often guess a number and think something like this - the answer must be just under 5,000 - I don't try to do a calculation that might get me the perfect answer.

All I want to do is check what answer the person gives me. If they said the correct answer was 4,946, I would probably accept it, as it is close to what I expected. If they answered 2,004, then I would get worried and start asking them to explain their answer.

---

[28] Meg Whitman, Joan O'C Hamilton (2010). "The Power of Many: Values for Success in Business and in Life", p.60, Crown Business
[29] Sheryl Sandberg, Nell Scovell 2013. *Lean In: Women, Work, and the Will to Lead.* Knopf

THE LAW OF 78

There are two types of revenue: one-off revenues and recurring revenues. Let me give you an example. If you sell a bicycle, then the customer pays a one-off sum of money and that's it. The only way you can increase your revenue, if you only sell bicycles, is to sell more. However, each financial year you start the year at zero sales and have to do it all again.

Now let's look at a recurring revenue stream like a cable TV subscription. Let's imagine each customer pays £10 per month and a salesman signs up 100 new customers each month. The total revenue he signs up each month is 10x100 = £1,000 per month.

The first month our revenue is £1,000. But, the second month our revenue is £2,000, the third £3,000 etc. So long as the salesperson keeps signing up

£1,000 of subscription (or recurring) revenue each month then the business will continue to grow.

I ran businesses that always had at least 75% of their sales from recurring products and services for this very reason. The power of compound numbers is huge.

I know that if we launch a new recurring revenue (or subscription) product, at the start of the financial year, with new sales of £1,000 per month, then the revenue in year one will be £78,000.

How do I know that? Think about it - the first customers will bill for 12-months, the second set of customers will bill for 11 months that year. The next months' customers will only bill for 10 months. Customers signed upon in the last month of the year will only bill for one month.

$$12+11+10+9+8+7+6+5+4+3+2+1 = 78$$

MY MESSAGE IS SIMPLE

The 'law of 78' gives you a very quick way of calculating first year revenues from new recurring products. If the sales team told me they could sell on average £10,000 per month of recurring revenues, then I knew the full year would be £780,000.

Let's go back to my advice about guessing the answer before you ask a question - the law of 78 allows you to quickly guess what the answer should be if you are discussing first year sales of recurring revenue products.

Don't forget the lesson on rounding - if you think 78 is a bit precise then use 80 - the answer should be a bit less than that as you have rounded up.

THAT'S NOT WHAT I EXPECTED

This is a simple technique that I have used for years. It is incredibly useful if you use it regularly.

If you ask someone a question and the answer is a number – guess the answer before you ask the question.

Let's use an example to illustrate what I mean …

Let's suppose you guess the answer should be 100 and the person responds 232. That is a huge difference and there are only two outcomes. Either:

1. You have found an error – the answer really is 100 or close and the responder is doing something incorrect to get to an answer of 232, or,
2. The answer really is 232 and that means you do not understand how this subject works.

Whenever someone gives me an answer I do not expect, I ask them to explain, how they have calculated the answer?

If their answer does not make any sense (or they cannot explain) then you have probably found an error. If they explain confidently why the answer is, in this example, 232. Then you should listen carefully, because they understand the issue and you need to learn how it works.

That way I learn something every time.

Let's do it the other way around.

You ask the question, without guessing the answer, and the responder says 232. You have no idea whether that sounds right or not and haven't learned anything.

MY MESSAGE IS SIMPLE

Think before you speak.

This technique is potentially so valuable that I am going to ask you to try it in real life. Try it first without guessing the answer and you will quickly appreciate that you have no idea whether the answer you have been given is true or not?

Now ask the question my suggested way and guess the answer before you ask the question. The more you practice this technique the more it will come natural to you.

PS - Let me tell you a true story of how a friend used my own technique back on me ...

When I am doing things quickly, (and discussing very large numbers) I sometimes guess the wrong number of noughts in the answer.

I said to him, "Can you believe Pizza Express[30] at one point had about £1.2 billion in debt and they only had just over 600 restaurants? That's about £20 million each restaurant. That is a ridiculously high amount."

He said, "That's also not true. The answer is nearly £2 million (which is the correct maths). The reason why I knew you were wrong? Your answer wasn't possible. I guessed that answer and £20 million could not possibly have been true."

Embarrassed I burst out laughing. My own technique had found my own errors.

---

[30] Sabah Meddings, 13th October 2019. *Ailing Pizza Express left bloated by debt.* Sunday Times Business Section page 12

BEWARE OF SPURIOUS ACCURACY

I want to go back to the idea that great businesspeople do not need to be great at maths. However, in business you often have to look at spreadsheets. I am going to invent a case study that will show you some simple techniques, that make looking at a spreadsheet full of numbers, a lot easier.

In our imaginary case study, we are running a business selling ladies shoes We have to decide how many pairs of black stilettos we are going to have manufactured, by our shoe manufacturer, for the forthcoming season? We have asked our marketing team to suggest how many shoes we should buy.

There are two types of spreadsheets. Some need to be factually accurate. Others; are merely attempts to estimate something. This sales forecast for our black stiletto shoes, is an example.

Ian Fishwick

Any spreadsheet has lots of 'cells.' They are normally named by the column and row headings eg A1, B6, D12 etc. Let's ignore the cells that have nothing in them or have text. Let's concentrate on the cells with numbers in. These cells contain either numbers that have been typed in or calculations.

The numbers that have been typed in are the assumptions that have been used and this is where we should concentrate our discussion at the meeting.

Ask whoever has created the spreadsheet to colour the cells containing numbers (not calculations). I normally use orange because it reminds me of an 'amber warning'. Once the cells have been coloured in, count how many cells have been coloured in. Are there a lot of assumptions? In our imaginary case study, I am going to use five cells coloured orange ie containing assumptions.

The next step is to ask whoever created the spreadsheet to go through each orange coloured cell and tell you if we know that exact number, or, is it an estimate? Never forget that an estimate is a best guess.

In our case study we know two of the five numbers: the selling price of the shoes is £49.99, and we know that our manufacturer has quoted a cost of £25 per pair to make them. Change the colour of these cells from orange to green. Green means that we do not need to worry about these numbers. We now know that our profit per pair of shoes will be £49.99 less £25 = £24.99. [I have assumed no taxes to keep this case study simple].

This leaves us with three orange coloured cells. In our case study these will be:

1. Market size - estimate (best guess) 100,000 pairs of stiletto shoes

2. Our market share we expect - best guess = 4.5%

3. Percentage of stiletto shoes that will be black and brown - best guess = 59% black, 41% brown

The number of black stiletto shoes we are expecting to sell this season is 100,000 x 4.5% x 59% = 2,655

The profit we are expecting to make from black stiletto shoes is 2,655 pairs x £24.99 profit per pair = £66,348.45

MY MESSAGE IS SIMPLE

If someone walks into a meeting and tells you that we are going to make exactly £66,348.45 profit from black stiletto shoes this season, then you immediately know that this is not possible. Forget what the spreadsheet says. We know that they are trying to guess what is going to happen, so it is

impossible to be that accurate. This is what I mean by 'spurious accuracy'.

In this example we identified three orange cells ie guesses. A guess added to a guess is a bigger guess. However ...

A guess multiplied by another guess and then multiplied by another guess ends up with a very big guess.

In our case study example, you do not need to understand how to create spreadsheets. You simply want a discussion on the three key assumptions. Why did they use these guesses for market size, market share and percentage of black shoes? Do we have historical data from previous seasons to tell us that these are sensible guesses or are have we never done this before, and we are totally guessing?

The more you do this, the more likely it is that your guesses, (or estimates) will get closer to reality. Be very wary of taking big decisions if it is the first time you have estimated something.

In practice I would have asked what the minimum order quantity was and how long it took the factory to manufacture some more shoes? It might reduce the risk if we bought less to start with and then ordered more later. Even if it put up the cost of the shoes it might be a less risky approach; until we get more market historical data.

CHAPTER EIGHT
Accounting and Finance

AN EASY WAY TO FIND OPERATIONAL PROCESS PROBLEMS

The Finance team? They are just the people who sit in the corner and add up invoices and shout at you if your expenses are submitted late. Aren't they? No, I don't see the Finance team that way at all.

Those readers who have had the dubious joy of being in lots of Finance reviews with me, will understand that one of the most common phrases I use is: what does that tell us about our processes? People probably do not expect me to talk regularly about processes in Finance meetings, but it is often the easiest place to spot broken or missing processes. Why is that? Most costs in a business follow one of two patterns: they are either the same, or very similar, each month, or they go up and down with sales revenues. When a cost does not follow these patterns that often means there is a problem. As ever let's use some examples to illustrate this.

Travel expenses

If you see a huge jump in travel expenses one month this may mean that people do not submit expense claims regularly and you have just received several months at once. There could be a genuine reason for this eg a sales conference, but if there is no obvious explanation then you have probably found a problem. It is very difficult to understand what your typical monthly costs are if staff do not submit their expense claims regularly.

Revenues and Costs

At one of our businesses we spotted that the cost of one product line rose, but the sales revenues did not. For many products there is no automated reconciliation of costs from suppliers with charges to customers. This simple cost change told me that we did not do a regular reconciliation. Do not underestimate how lengthy this task can be or how beneficial it can be. The exercise took several weeks but revealed all sorts of problems.

- One supplier was still charging us for things that we had cancelled months before
- We were charging customers for products that had been ordered but not installed yet
- Some products had been sold at very low margins

At the end of the exercise our profitability improved considerably.

Not Charging for Stuff You should Charge For

We spotted that one of our businesses had unusually low professional fee charges from the service desk. At times we can be too helpful. If a customer has a problem on say Saturday, but only pays for Monday to Friday 8am to 6pm cover; what do you do? Some people simply fix the problem anyway. The correct answer is to explain the service levels they are paying for and ask politely whether they can wait until Monday morning or whether they want to pay an out of hours charge to have the problem fixed immediately? This simple process change improved the profitability of one of our businesses by over £50,000 per year – enough to pay for more people on the service desk.

MY MESSAGE IS SIMPLE

Don't just look at numbers. Think about what they mean. Numbers tell stories.

PLAY CHESS NOT DRAUGHTS

My late brother, Chris used to say, "We are all playing on the same board, but some businesses are playing draughts and others are playing chess."

What did he mean by this?

Draughts is a relatively simple game and people often only look to their next move. Chess is much more complex and involves analysing a range of options, and more importantly, thinking several moves ahead. He was clearly encouraging us to constantly look further ahead.

The way that we did it was this: every Monday morning for the 16 years I was CEO (and it carried on afterwards with the new CEO) we would re-forecast our financial results for this year and next year. Surely not, I hear you say? That must be so difficult and time consuming?

The opposite is true. It is very simple, and very quick. The way we did it was this ...

We had a weekly executive directors meeting with a standard agenda. That is nothing new. However, at the end, we asked the simple question "what has changed since last Monday?" By asking the question religiously every week, the changes we had to remember were few. They were also small. For example, it could be as simple as a person left last week, or someone started.

We then input that change to our financial model. The rule was that only one thing could be changed at once. We then kept a list of the changes and the impact it had. Over time it allowed us to instinctively know which changes had a big financial impact on our business eg last month's new orders from customers (and how it compared to our previous forecast).

We then finished the meeting by looking at the new financial forecast for this year and next year.

MY MESSAGE IS SIMPLE

The sooner you spot a problem, the more time you have to find a solution or take other action. As an example - if the sales team have had a quiet few months' then it may be necessary to slow down recruitment and control your costs.

If you find a problem at the last minute there is very little you can do about it. The senior management team could see that we didn't take sudden panic measures. They understood the way we worked, and everyone pulled together if we spotted a problem early.

THE ONE-SIDE-OF-A4 BUSINESS PLAN

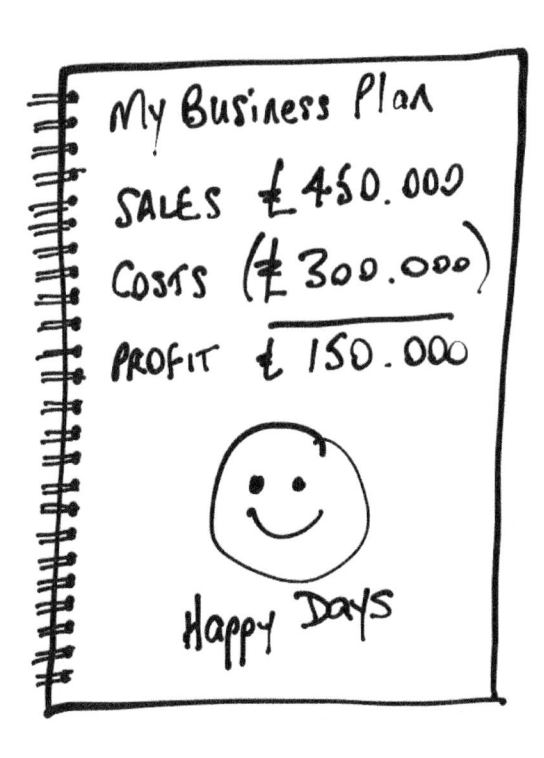

My Business Plan

SALES £450,000
COSTS (£300,000)
PROFIT £150,000

Happy Days

In business discussions I often hear people talk about 'fag packets.' The phrase is often used to describe an idea explained simply on the back of a cigarette packet. I have never smoked and there is virtually no room to write anything on a cigarette packet. I therefore prefer the phrase 'master one-side of A4'.

What do I mean?

If you have an idea for setting up a business, then try to write a summary of the Business Plan on a single side of A4 paper. I don't mean write a wordy explanation of your idea. I mean the key financial numbers. If you cannot explain how you are going to make money very simply then the business probably won't work.

Let me do an imaginary example of a plan for a restaurant ...

Startup costs ...

- Fit-out including kitchen £25,000
- Website (needed for bookings) £5,000
- TOTAL START-UP COSTS £30,000

Annual forecasts

You will need to make some assumptions ...

- 200 Meals sold per week at average £45 (after removing VAT) = £9,000
- Assume open for 50 weeks a year = 50 weeks x £9,000 = £450,000
- Food and drink costs 1/3 of selling price = £450,000/3 = £150,000

Forecast Profit and Loss account ...

- £450,000 - Sales of food and drink
- (£150,000) - cost of food and drink
- £300,000 - Margin on food and drink
- (£100,000) - 2 staff in kitchen + 3 front of house = 5 at average salary of £20,000 each
- (£13,800) - Payroll taxes (national insurance in the UK) 13.8%
- (£100,000) - Rent and rates
- £86,200 profit before tax

Note that I have put the costs in brackets to make them easier to spot.

MY MESSAGE IS SIMPLE

This example is over-simplified. I am simply trying to show you that it is possible to make a profit on a restaurant like this. However, we can already see that there is a limit to how much money it can make because the sales are not that much higher than the costs. Having said that, if you want to run a restaurant, because that is your passion, then you can clearly make a living doing that. Assuming that all your forecasts for sales and costs are correct.

Don't forget that forecasts are just 'guesses.' Change your guesses a bit to see if your plan still works. Always remember that it is easier to predict costs than sales. You are much more likely to guess correctly the number of people you will employ and what you will pay them. You can look up the rent and rates. How many meals you can sell is much more of a guess.

If you only sold 100 meals per week, rather than 200, your margin is halved to £150,000 and you will lose money.

If you sell 300 meals, rather than 200, then your margin goes up to £450,000 and you will make much more money.

When your costs are relatively fixed, you need to understand, how different volumes can easily affect you?

If your business plan doesn't pass this simple 'one-side of A4' test, then it is unlikely to succeed.

THE TOP-3-THINGS RULE

	My PRIORITIES	THIS YEAR	NEXT YEAR
1.	PRICE RISES	40	120
2.	CLOSE SECOND OFFICE	20	60
3.	DON'T REPLACE ONE LEAVER	15	45
4.	Not so important	10	22
5.	Nice To Have	—	—
6.	Another Nice To Have	—	—

One of the biggest problems about being about a boss, or even worse the ultimate boss, the CEO, is that no-one tells you what to do each day, week or month. There is no simple guidebook, that tells you what to do at 10am every morning or the second Tuesday of the month. It is up to you. Some people relish this choice as freedom. Others get paralysed by it like a rabbit in a headlight.

Some business owners get to a point where their team can run the business day-to-day and they go off playing golf. If they own the business, then this is their prerogative. If they are employees, then this should not be happening.

Be very wary of continually thinking of new ideas and strategies as this is extremely difficult for staff to handle. I recall listening to a famous politician many years ago, but I can't remember who it was. He had an interesting point to make. He said something like this.

"These young politicians look at the old fat blokes like me with disdain. They see us as the old duffers who have lunch every day, but we were much more effective at getting things done. We would spend a long time discussing what to do and then after we had briefed the civil servants we would go for lunch, every day, for weeks. It stopped us thinking of new ideas when they hadn't had a chance to implement the last one yet."

He was arguing his case in an extreme way and I'm certainly not advocating that approach for all senior managers. However, he did have a very good point about initiative overload. I worried about this issue quite a lot. If I was only going to encourage the senior management team to concentrate on a few things; how do you decide what they are?

Every few weeks I would find a quiet place and sit on my own. I would write a list of all the things I thought we should be working on. Once I had stopped writing the list, I would look at how many items there were. Some weeks the list was much longer than others.

I would then write two columns next to each item on the list. The headings were 'This Year' and 'Next Year'. I would guess the financial impact of fixing that item on the list. I would normally try to express it in monthly terms.

Let's imagine that one item on the list could save us £10,000 per month (don't forget this is a rough guess). If there were four months of this financial year to go, I would write £40,000 under 'This Year' and £120,000 under 'Next Year'.

I would then re-order the list in descending value order. The things that could improve profitability the most were at the top. Because the list has to be re-ordered like this it is often easier to do it on a computer rather than a piece of paper.

I would then look again at the list and see which of the items the team were already working on. If you do this you will often find that people are working on important things, but they are sixth or seventh on the list and no-one is working on some of the top three items.

MY MESSAGE IS SIMPLE

The more initiatives you have the more you stretch the team. The more likely it is that they are working on things that are not the most important and are 'nice to have'.

If you cannot guess the financial implication of doing something on your list, then you should sit down with your finance person and ask them to guess the answer. I did this all the time with my Finance Director. This is how you get the best value out of the accounts team.

I have often seen senior managers arguing that they have been incredibly busy in the last year and they have achieved some great things, but they are still being criticised. This often means that their financial results are poor, and they have not been working on the top three things that could have given the best financial improvement.

CHAPTER NINE
Bank Borrowing

BANKS SELL MONEY

Before we start to look at business bank lending in detail, I want to tell you a story.

When we first started to borrow money, from Barclays, our Client Relationship Director asked to meet the team. Our Sales Director asked him 'how much commission do you make when you sell a loan and what are your sales targets"?

As well as enjoying the Barclays mans' face, as he was taken aback by the question, I realised that I had just learned something really important. Many of us, me included up to that point, see banks as the people who say, 'No.' The reality is the opposite. They are a business selling a service like any other business. It just happens that their service is lending money.

If they do not lend money, then they, do not make any profit. They therefore need to say, 'Yes' to people who want to borrow money or they cannot survive.

Do not be confused, because banks do not employ anyone, with the job title of sales. Your account manager or Client Relationship Director is a salesperson in all but name.

The difference with banks is that they need checks and balances to ensure the 'sales team' do not lend money recklessly. All proposals are therefore sent to the Credit Committee. The Credit Committee must live in a black hole somewhere as they never seem to see daylight - this is a fairly common joke - as the Credit Committee tend to operate from a bank office and rarely come out to visit customers. This is partly for convenience and partly because they do not want to be influenced by meeting the customer. Their decisions are made simply on the financial information presented to them.

The Credit Committee will do a credit check on your firm and also review your business plan or financial forecasts to see how believable they are and how they stand up to worst case scenarios.

MY MESSAGE IS SIMPLE

Banks want to lend you money, so long as you can show that you can repay the loan. I have always found that the best approach is to be open with the bank about your business objectives and where they fit into the plan. The more they know about your business the better.

One year, when I was Chairman, I asked our Chief Executive to invite our bankers to our Sales Conference. He was understandably wary about inviting external banks into an internal meeting which would show us warts and all. Many of the agenda items at the Sales Conference were very positive - big contract wins, new products etc - but there was also a discussion about things we could do better. The Chief Executive reluctantly agreed.

At the end of the sales conference, our banks (as we had several) came to us absolutely beaming with enthusiasm. "No-one has ever invited us in to see a real meeting before. The atmosphere is brilliant. This is so impressive. We now understand why you love this business."

When you talk to a bank, be confident about your business, whilst being realistic.

SHOULD I BORROW FROM A BANK?

Most businesses, at some point, ask themselves whether they should borrow money from a bank? I think there are a range of questions you should ask yourself before you even think of bank lending.

Let me explain with an example from your personal life.

Would anyone consider taking out a 3-year loan to pay for a restaurant meal? I hope not. The idea of having to pay every month for the next three years, for a meal that you have already long forgotten, seems somewhat ridiculous. However, the idea of taking out a 3-year loan to buy a car seems sensible. The idea of taking out a 25-year mortgage to buy a house seems pretty standard. The key point here is that the type of loan you take out depends on what you are buying and the expected life of that asset. A car will definitely last three years, but it would almost certainly struggle to last 25-years.

So, in business you need to start with a clear understanding of what you need the money for? Am I buying a short, medium or long-term asset? That will tell you what type of financing you should consider. Do not forget that borrowing from a bank is only one possible source of the money you need.

Start by looking at your existing business. If you did things better could you generate some money? If, for example, your debtors (monies owed to you by customers) are too high, the simple act of collecting money from your customers will generate some cash. If you have stocks of products; can you sell them to raise some cash?

You can issue new equity - ask investors (including yourself) to buy new shares in your business. This involves an emotional question: do you want complete control or are you prepared to own a smaller portion of your business if it helps it to grow more quickly?

If you want money to fund the day-to-day activities of the business, then you might look at getting a bank overdraft. In situations where customers routinely take quite a long time to pay their bills, then it might be worth considering 'invoice discounting'. We will look at both of these types of finance in the section on cashflow lending.

When individuals are borrowing money, the sad reality is that poor people pay higher interest on their loans than rich people do. The chances of a rich person repaying the loan is higher than a poorer one. The way a lender covers the increased chance of not being re-paid is to charge higher interest. The same thing happens in the business world: the better your credit score, the lower your interest rate and vice versa.

MY MESSAGE IS SIMPLE

How you pay for something is a secondary question. The starting point should be: what do you need the money for?

Do not forget that it is much easier to spend money than earn it, so never discount the idea of simply not spending the money at all.

If you are going to go down the route of bank borrowing, then you need an understanding of what that involves. Over the next few sections I will try to cover the basics.

HOW DOES BANK LENDING WORK? THE BASICS

In our look at the basics of business borrowing, let's start by examining what kind of costs are involved, when businesses borrow money. If you want a loan, then you will have to pay some upfront costs. Banks typically charge an administration fee for arranging your loan. This can be anywhere from 1.0-2.5% of the value of the loan. The more you are borrowing and the longer your track record, of repaying money to the bank on time, the more likely you are to have administration charges at the lower end of that range. If you are new to business borrowing, then expect higher charges.

There will be a formal contract or 'loan agreement' outlining the terms of your loan. You will need to pay your solicitors to review the loan agreement. This next bit has always seemed to be unfair to me: the bank will need to hire lawyers to draw up the loan agreement and you will often be asked to pay for the banks' lawyers (as well as your own). Their argument is that they wouldn't need a lawyer if you didn't want to borrow money. My argument (which has never been accepted) is that the bank makes money on the loan, so it is in their interests to appoint (and pay for) their own lawyers. Unfortunately, these costs mount up. As there is often a similar amount of work for lawyers in drawing up a loan agreement, regardless of the amount borrowed, it can be very expensive to borrow a small amount of money.

There are two main types of loans: repayment loans and interest-only loans. With a repayment loan you pay back interest and part of the amount borrowed each month. The amount you owe the bank therefore reduces with every repayment; normally monthly. With an interest-only loan you pay the interest every month, but only repay the amount borrowed at the end. If, at the end of the loan period, you do not want to repay the outstanding amount, then you often have the option to agree another interest-only loan and effectively postpone the date for repaying the loan. Every time you extend the loan you will be charged administration and lawyers' fees again.

There is another variation on this: a loan where nothing is repaid until the end. The interest is calculated each month and added to the total amount outstanding. This type of loan is only normally available to experienced borrowers. As the bank is getting no money at all, until the end, the risk is much higher. Therefore, the interest rates can be much higher.

MY MESSAGE IS SIMPLE

Do not make the mistake of just looking at the interest rate. There are bound to be upfront costs, although you might be able to get the bank to add them to the loan, rather than pay them upfront. Even more important: do not make the mistake of thinking that you can do what you want with the money. Just think about it for a minute - if you borrow money to build a warehouse, the bank does not what to find out that you bought say, a racehorse instead. The bank will insist that you send them monthly management accounts, so that they can see how close you are to your original forecasts, that you sent them, when you negotiated the loan. There will also be restrictions written into your loan agreement explaining how you are allowed to use the money. I ran a business that historically only spent an amount each year, equivalent to 1% of sales, on capital expenditure. To ensure I did not change our business model without the banks' agreement, they placed a limit on how much we could spend each year on capital expenditure, without their permission.

The restrictions placed on you will be specific to your business. That is why all loan agreements are slightly different. They are also quite lengthy documents; ours were over 170 pages. The loan agreement will also explain the 'redemption charges' if you want to repay the loan early.

WHEN YOU NEED MORE THAN ONE BANK

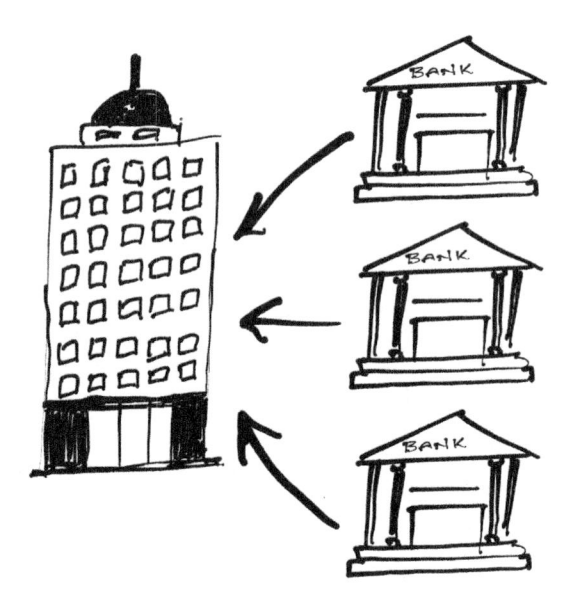

Many people, in their private life, have more than one credit card. Let's imagine you have two credit cards, and both have a credit limit of £2,000. In total you have a £4,000 credit limit. Why didn't you just have one credit card with a £4,000 limit on it? Wouldn't that be easier to manage?

The simple answer is that the decision was not up to you. The credit card companies saw you as a risk in that you may not pay the loan back and they did not want to take all that risk themselves. Instead they split the risk between them, taking £2,000 each. This is the maximum they would lend you.

In this example, the credit card companies did not say that you should not be given a £4,000 loan. They simply said that they wanted to share the risk with some other lender.

The same thing happens in business.

Let's imagine there were only two companies in town, and they were similar, so they both justified a £20 million loan. If there were only two banks in town, then it is unlikely they would want to have a £20 million with one of the companies and nothing with the other company. It would be much less risky for them if the two banks lent £10 million each to both companies. This spreads their risk. If one of the two companies hit a problem, then their money at risk is smaller.

Let's now scale this example to the whole of the economy. Once a business loan gets to a certain size, the banks may decide that they want to set up a multi-bank club or 'syndicate'. It does not mean you won't get your loan it just means that all lenders will have to agree to the same loan agreement, which is often more difficult as you have several sets of lawyers involved. Not surprisingly, legal costs for multi-bank loans are often higher because of the amount of work involved.

MY MESSAGE IS SIMPLE

As your business loans get bigger you should expect your bank to suggest that other banks should start to share the risk. Talk to your bank account manager and ask them at what size of loan this is likely to happen.

The longer you have to make friends, with a second or third bank, the better. For many years our only bank was Barclays. I was a speaker at RBS Nat West technology events for about a decade before I rang them one day to ask them if they fancied becoming our second bank in a loan arrangement. The conversation was much easier because we had known each other for years.

Look ahead and plan accordingly.

WHAT IS ASSET-BACKED LENDING?

The easiest type of bank lending to understand is asset-backed lending. Think of a mortgage on your house. The bank takes a charge over the house, so if you do not repay your mortgage, they can get their money back by forcing you to sell your house and using the proceeds to repay their loan.

Asset-backed lending is similar, except the bank wants you to put up some asset eg a building, as security, so that they have something to sell if you do not repay the loan. In business your 'assets' are not just buildings. They effectively include anything that can be sold to raise money to repay the loan if needed. This includes things like stock, debtors and even Intellectual Property. Whenever you get a loan agreement from a bank you will normally see that they want a charge over all your assets.

Once you have given a lender a charge over all your assets it becomes more difficult to borrow money from someone else. If you try to borrow more money, then the second lender will only get their money back when the bank with the first charge over all your assets, has got their money back first. That means the second lender is clearly taking a bigger risk.

Sometimes they simply will not lend you any money because of the perceived risk. However, if they do decide to lend you money and become what is known as 'secondary debt' then the way a bank tries to counter the higher risk is by charging you a higher interest rate. You can therefore end up with a number of loans all paying different interest rates.

The difficulty here is that many small businesses do not own any assets. That is why many banks ask for personal guarantees. That way if you do not repay the loan, they can force you to sell your house, or whatever else you own. My advice is to avoid personal guarantees wherever possible. It is one thing losing your business if it fails. It is quite another to lose your home and everything you own; especially if you have a family to look after.

In the next section we will look at another form of bank-lending - cashflow lending.

MY MESSAGE IS SIMPLE

A bank wherever possible, will want some form of security, so that they have something they can sell if you do not repay the loan. Ensure that you are careful about what security you offer eg if your total assets were £1 million, but the loan was only £100,000, then find an asset worth say £150,000 (a bit more than the loan). Be careful of pledging security over all your assets as it restricts your ability to borrow in the future. Being perfectly honest - this is easier said than done as banks are not the easiest to negotiate with if they can sense that you are desperate for the money.

Ironically, it is sometimes easier to borrow money when you do not need it.

BORROWING AGAINST INTELLECTUAL PROPERTY

Some finance companies, Lombard are a good example, based their business on lending businesses money to buy physical things like machinery in factories. The problem they have, is that not as much money is spent these days, on physical equipment. We live in a world where apps and software are much more common. Often owning the Intellectual Property of a piece of software is the only major asset a company has.

The lenders are now realising this and are starting to come up with ways that will allow you to borrow money against Intellectual Property for software.

When you are financing a physical asset such as a machine, you know what it cost, as you can see the invoice. It is not that straightforward for a piece of software. So, how do the bank lenders decide how much they can lend you?

The lender will look at three things:

1. How much did it cost you to develop the software? This is one of the reasons why you should think about tracking the hours spent by your software engineers developing something. If a person is full-time on a software development, then calculating the cost of development is a bit easier.

2. The second thing the lender will look at is how much the software is worth? If you tried to sell the software to another company, how much are they likely to pay? For a new company with a new piece of software this may be very difficult to calculate with any accuracy.

3. The third option is to look at the revenues being generated by the software and forecast the cashflows they will generate. They then produce a 'discounted cash flow' (DCF). A DCF attempts to recognise the time value of money eg £1 in 10-years' time is worth less than £1 today. This valuation only works if the software is generating revenues.

MY MESSAGE IS SIMPLE

If you are a software company it is worth looking for a specialist company, such as Lombard, who offer loans against Intellectual Property. You are more likely to be successful in persuading them to lend you money if the software is already generating revenues. If you think about it this is only fair as there are loads of people developing interesting software that is clever, but no-one is prepared to pay money to use.

WHAT IS CASHFLOW LENDING?

Many companies are based in a rented or leased office. They sell services, so their offices all look similar - rows of desks with PC's and laptops on them. The similarity extends to their banking problems - they do not own any physical assets, so have nothing that the bank can sell, as you would with typical asset-backed lending.

In 2018, the 'services' sector represented 81% of the UK economy.[31] The banks therefore have to find a way of lending to companies who have no, or minimal, assets. If they didn't then they would be ignoring the vast bulk of the

---

[31] UK House of Commons Library, 2019 *Service Industries: Key economic Indicators* [online]. Available at:
<https://researchbriefings.parliament.uk/ResearchBriefing/Summary/SN02786> [Accessed on 13 December 2019]

UK's companies.

There are some options for bank borrowing if you do not have any assets. Collectively they are known as 'cashflow' lending.

An overdraft should be seen as a way of 'tiding you over' until your customers pay. It often works well if you have to pay your suppliers before you get paid from your customers. In this type of scenario, the faster you grow, the more cash you will need. The problem with overdrafts is that banks can ask for their money back whenever they want, with very little notice. Overdrafts are therefore only suitable for financing short-term things.

If you go back to our original analogy in a previous section - an overdraft might be ok to pay for a meal, but it certainly is not an acceptable way of buying a house over say 25 years.

If you have a business where your customers regularly take a long time to pay, then you might consider 'invoice discounting'. Most banks have specialist departments that do this. The principle is straightforward: instead of the customer paying you in say, three months' time, the bank pays your invoices now. They deduct a fee for giving you the money early. Is it worth paying a fee to get the cash early? You would need to have a good look at the costs and benefits. Do not forget that you will need to set up special systems to manage an 'invoice discounting' facility.

How does a bank decide how much your business can afford to borrow? Let's again use an example from your personal life to explain the principles.

If you borrow money to buy a car then the lender wants to understand whether you are likely to be able to afford it. It is a fairly simple concept: after paying for your normal monthly costs, how much money do you have left and is that enough to repay the loan comfortably?

The same concept is used for service companies. How much profit do they normally have after paying all their costs? Is any of the cash generated from the profits (after tax) normally used to pay for other things such as regular capital expenditure? Once you have established how much free cash you have available then you have an idea how much you can afford to use for interest and loan repayments.

In your private life, if you get the same salary every month, then it is easier to plan your finances as you know how much money you have to spend. In business it is not as simple and predictable as that: profits can go up and down, so you will probably need to forecast several scenarios showing how much cash you have available if things go wrong. Often people do three forecasts: a base case (what you think is going to happen), a worst case (if sales are say 10% lower) and a best case (where sales are 10% higher). Only you can decide whether 10% is the appropriate amount for a best and worst case.

A bank will typically want to lend against a conservative profit forecast. It is pointless telling a bank that you normally make £500,000 a year, but next year, and every year thereafter, it will be double (unless you have an extremely good reason for saying that).

To borrow money using a cashflow forecast you normally need several years of trading history; so that the bank can see what normal looks like. This means it might take you several years before you can use this kind of lending.

MY MESSAGE IS SIMPLE

The longer a business has been trading the easier it should be to borrow money, so long as it is profitable. Banks are conservative and prefer to be able to forecast what is likely to happen with a reasonable degree of comfort. A track record is therefore important.

I hope this section has shown that it is possible to borrow money even if you do not own any assets. I ran a service company for years. We started with an overdraft, then moved to an invoice discounting facility. We paid off the invoice discounting facility as soon as we had a long enough track record to borrow money on a three, or five-year, loan.

WHY INTEREST RATES ARE NEVER AS LOW AS YOU EXPECT

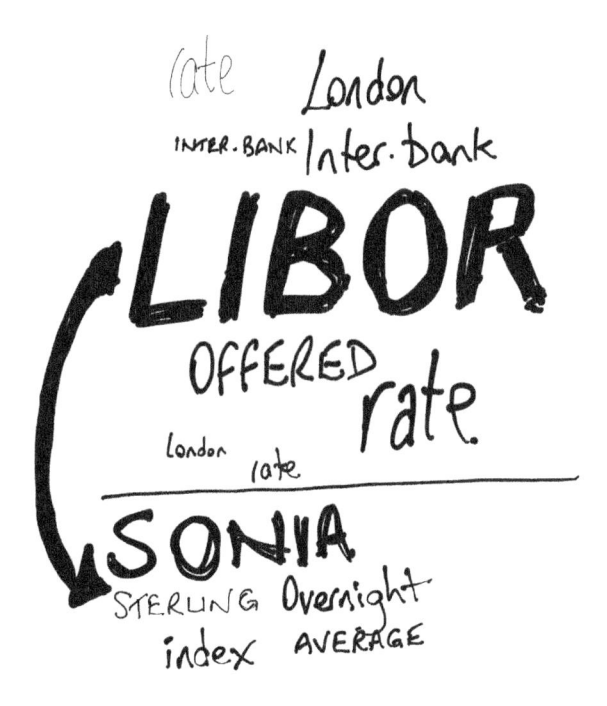

LIBOR (London Interbank Offered rate)

SONIA (Sterling Overnight Index Average)

When people first start borrowing money, they often expect the interest rate they will be charged to be lower than it actually is. Why is that?

If you listen to the news and you hear an announcement that says something like "The Monetary Policy Committee at the Bank of England has kept interest rates unchanged at 0.75%" then some people assume that this is what they are going to pay. Unfortunately, it is not.

Most loan agreements will say that the interest percentage applicable to your loan is an amount known as the banks margin plus LIBOR.

The London Interbank Offered Rate (LIBOR) is a benchmark interest rate at which major global banks lend to one another in the international interbank market for short-term loans.

Let's start with a simple example.

If the bank margin you are being charged is 3.0% and LIBOR is 0.75% then you will be charged 3.75% interest. If LIBOR moves up to 1.0% then you will pay (3+1) = 4%. Conversely if interest rates dropped and LIBOR became 0.5% then you would pay 3.5%.

Let's go back to your private life. If you have a mortgage to buy a property, the amount you were allowed to borrow will have been calculated as a multiple of your salary. The size of the mortgage is not the issue - some people can afford to borrow more than others because they earn a lot more. The issue is the salary multiple. Someone borrowing twice their salary is much less risky than someone borrowing five times their salary. It is similar in business.

Unfortunately, the acronym EBITDA is going to feature quite a lot in this section on banking, so let's try to understand why it is important. EBITDA stands for Earnings Before Interest Tax and Depreciation. Think of it as Operating Profit. Assuming that you collect all the cash owed by your customers and pay all your suppliers, then this is the amount of operating cashflow your business generates. How much money does your business make before you have to pay for taxes and bank interest?

The more EBITDA (or Operating Profit) you make, the more you can borrow.

Someone borrowing a sum equivalent to one years' EBITDA (or Operating Profit) is much less risky than someone borrowing three years EBITDA.

When you are borrowing over longer terms - let's use five years as our example - the banks will sometimes vary their 'margin' depending upon how high your borrowing ratio is. The 'Leverage ratio' is your borrowing divided by your annual EBITDA. So, for example, if you have borrowed £2.5 million and your EBITDA per annum is £1 million, then your 'leverage ratio' is 2.5.

This is an imaginary example to illustrate the point:

If your Leverage Ratio is 2.5 or greater then, the margin is 3% per annum. If your Leverage Ratio is between 2.0 and 2.5 then the margin is 2.75%. Imagine that every time the Leverage Ratio drops by 0.5 then the margin drops by 0.25%. It can't drop forever, so it stops at a point where if Leverage Ratio is less than 1.0 then the margin is 2.0%.

What often happens is that your 'leverage ratio' is highest at the start of the loan; when you have just borrowed the money. As you earn profits and repay some of the loan, the 'leverage ratio' gets lower over time and in the later years your interest rate drops.

MY MESSAGE IS SIMPLE

The interest rate you pay will not be LIBOR. It will be LIBOR plus the banks' margin. The banks' margin may vary depending on how high your leverage ratio is I.e. how risky you are as a borrower.

PS - please note that LIBOR is being phased out and will be replaced by SONIA. The concepts in this article will remain the same it is simply that the value will be SONIA rather than LIBOR. So, what is SONIA?

Most of the major business banks are explaining this change to their customers. My notes were taken from Santander.

In April 2017, in the UK, the Working Group on Sterling Risk-Free Reference Rates (the RFR Working Group) recommended SONIA – the Sterling Overnight Index Average – as its preferred alternative reference interest rate for sterling transactions.

BANK COVENANTS - THE RULES YOU MUST OBEY

When you take out a mortgage to buy a house, there are certain rules attached to the loan. Often these rules explain what you are expected to do. As an example, you are supposed to keep the building in a good state of repair. When you borrow money for business use there are normally more rules. These rules are often referred to as bank covenants.

Banks do not want to find out at the last minute that you cannot repay their loan, as they then have to quickly intervene, to try to get their money back. They may have to force the sale of some of the companies' assets, or in a worst case, take over the business. Instead, they want early warning, that things are not looking good. This way they have time to discuss options with the company, whilst there is still time to do so. No-one wants to find out there is a problem when it is too late to do anything about it.

Let us imagine that in your private life, you had borrowed money for a mortgage on the basis of three times your salary. If you lose your job then your repayments are at risk and the sooner you have a discussion with the lender, the more likely they are to help you find a solution. As an example, they might extend the period of the loan to give you more time to pay it back.

It works in a similar way with business loans: the 'bank covenants' are intended to be early warning signals for a bank.

Each month you will be required to send your management accounts to the bank. This enables the bank to check how you are doing against the business plan cashflow forecast that you submitted when you borrowed the money. It also allows them to check whether you are operating inside the 'rules' or covenants. So, what are these covenants?

Your business loan agreement will contain a number of covenants. I am going to look at the two most common ones: EBITDA : Net Debt leverage ratio and Interest Cover.0

First of all, let's ensure that you understand what I mean by 'net debt'. Net debt is the amount you have borrowed less any cash balances you hold, so if you have borrowed £2.5 million but have £100,000 cash in the bank then your 'net debt' is £2.4 million.

Let us imagine that the bank has set a covenant that says you cannot borrow more than three years EBITDA. If last year you made £1 million in EBITDA then the maximum you would be able to borrow is £3 million. That does not mean you have to borrow £3 million. It simply means that this is the most that you can borrow.

Let us imagine that you have borrowed £2.4 million. If your EBITDA is £1 million per annum, then your leverage ratio is 2.4 (£2.4 million Net Debt divided by £1 million EBITDA).

In a previous section we discussed the problem that in a business profits can go up and down. If the year after, your EBITDA has fallen to £600,000, but your net Debt is still £2.4 million then we have a problem. Your leverage ratio is now 4 (£2.4 million divided by £600,000). Once you go higher than your maximum bank covenant (in our example, 3), the bank has the right to intervene and sell some of your assets or take control of your business.

The second most common covenant is Interest Cover. The bank wants to know that you can comfortably pay back the interest on the loan. If you cannot afford to pay the interest, how are you going to be able to afford to repay the loan itself?

The way the bank keeps an eye on this is by comparing your EBITDA to your interest charges. Normally banks want your interest cover to be above four.

Let's do an example ...

If your EBITDA is £1 million and your interest charges are £200,000 then your interest cover is £1 million divided by £200,000 = 5. So, the bank will say that is fine.

Let us continue with our example we used previously where EBITDA fell to £600,000 but debt did not change and therefore the interest charge would stay the same at £200,000. The interest cover is now 3 (£600,000 EBITDA divided by £200,000 interest). This breaks your interest cover covenant (of 4x) and the bank can now sell some or all of your assets.

MY MESSAGE IS SIMPLE

You never want to get into a situation where the bank forces you to sell some of your assets, or even worse takes over your business completely. It is therefore really important that you understand how your bank covenants work and what would trigger the banks taking control. You must avoid this at all costs.

You therefore need to ensure that you check carefully the management accounts that you send the bank each month. These accounts must show you are operating well within your bank covenants. However, this is not enough. Your management accounts tell you what has already happened. You need to spot any looming problem before it arises.

This is why forecasting is so important if you decide to borrow money from banks. If you can see that you are getting too close for comfort with your bank covenants, then you need time to take action.

You may need to boost your EBITDA quickly. Often this can mean a painful cost cutting exercise where you may have to get rid of staff, many of whom may be friends. This is not ideal, but it is still preferable to the bank taking control of your business.

If you look like you may be heading for trouble, then you should also consider doing anything that will keep your debt down. Do not make the mistake of spending a lot of money on Capital Expenditure, say a new fleet of vans, just before you hit a problem.

If you don't have the patience for financial forecasting, then either get an accountant who can help you, or stay away from bank borrowing.

REVOLVING CREDIT FACILITIES AND ACCORDIONS

We are now going to move on to slightly more sophisticated types of bank borrowing: Revolving Credit Facilities (RCFs) and Accordions. As ever, let's start with an example from your private life.

Let's think about credit cards. I can't believe I have just written that as I hate credit cards with a vengeance because of the high interest charges and the problems they cause many families. What I meant to say was 'let's look at the financial structure of credit cards and see if there is anything similar in the business world'.

A credit card has an agreed credit limit. Let's imagine that when you first got the credit card the limit on it was £2,000. However, you have now had the card for several years and you have never missed a payment, so the credit limit has been gradually increased to £5,000. You can spend the money on whatever you want, and you do not need to ask the banks permission before you do so. Each month you have three choices: you can pay off the whole of the loan, pay back a minimum amount (which is mainly interest) or some value between the two. There is no time limit on a credit card. It normally carries on, so long as you keep up with the payments, or pay off the loan. You only pay interest on the amount you have spent.

Now let's look at a special type of business loan known as a Revolving Credit Facility (RCF). It is similar to a credit card in that you are given a credit limit. Let's use £5 million for our example.

There are several differences to how a credit card works. First, you can only use the money for whatever purpose was agreed in your loan agreement. Second, there is a fixed period, say 5 years. Third, you pay interest each month, but only pay back the loan at the end of the period. Fourth, you pay interest on the money you have not used as well as the amount you have spent. What I hear you say? How does that work? Let me show you with an example …

The banks argument is that they have allocated you £5 million, so they cannot now lend to that to anyone else. I would love to see the shelf where my unborrowed money is kept, but it doesn't work like that. Let's assume you have borrowed £4 million and have £1 million still available to borrow from your £5 million credit limit.

You will be charged the full interest rate (bank margin plus LIBOR) on the borrowed amount. However, you will also be charged a % of the bank margin on the undrawn amount (in this example the £1 million). Often this can be around 40% of the normal interest rate. Let's do a calculated example assuming LIBOR is 0.5%, the bank interest rate is 3% and the charge for undrawn funds is 40%.

Your borrowings of £4 million will be charged at an interest rate of 3.5% (bank margin plus LIBOR). Your undrawn funds of £1 million will be charged at 40% x 3% bank margin = 1.2%

If you have to pay for money you have not borrowed yet, why would you do this?

The advantage of having a credit card is that the money is available to use whenever you wish. It is similar, although not quite as simple, with a Revolving Credit Facility. When we were buying companies regularly, we set up a Revolving Credit Facility, so that we knew what our credit limit was. Every time we found a company we wanted to buy, we sent a short 2 to 4-page paper to the bank and asked them to allow us to draw down the money.

This is much quicker than trying to negotiate a new loan agreement every time. We had to pay 40% of the interest on the money we had not borrowed yet, but it was a price worth paying. It meant we already knew we had the money available before we made an offer to buy a company. It was a bit like going shopping knowing that you have some money available on your credit card.

When using a Revolving Credit Facility, one of the key questions you have to ask yourself is: how much am I prepared to pay, for money I have not borrowed yet? If you set that value too high, then you can pay high amounts in interest without ever borrowing the money. One way round this problem is to use what is known as an 'accordion'.

Let us imagine that a bank has reviewed our business plan and is prepared to lend us up to £20 million, but we do not think we need to borrow that much yet. However, we may need the full amount at some point. We now need to decide how much we need to borrow now (let's say £10 million), how much we want undrawn on the Revolving Credit Facility (let's say £5 million) and then the balance of the £20 million (in this case £5 million) we can put on an accordion facility.

So, what is an accordion facility? To avoid having to negotiate another loan agreement, the bank agrees that the current documentation is fine to cover the whole £20 million. If they have taken a charge over all your assets you probably have no security left to give, so it would be pointless negotiating another loan agreement as nothing would change in the document. When you are ready to use the money on the accordion facility you simply notify the bank and so long as you are operating safely within your bank covenants, they will increase the size of your Revolving Credit Facility.

MY MESSAGE IS SIMPLE

Your bank account manager should be treated as part of your team. Talk to them regularly about how your business is going and what your plans for the future are. When I started, I had never heard of things like 'accordion facilities.' I always started by explaining the problem I was trying to solve and then asked the bank for ideas.

WHAT IS A CONVERTIBLE LOAN?

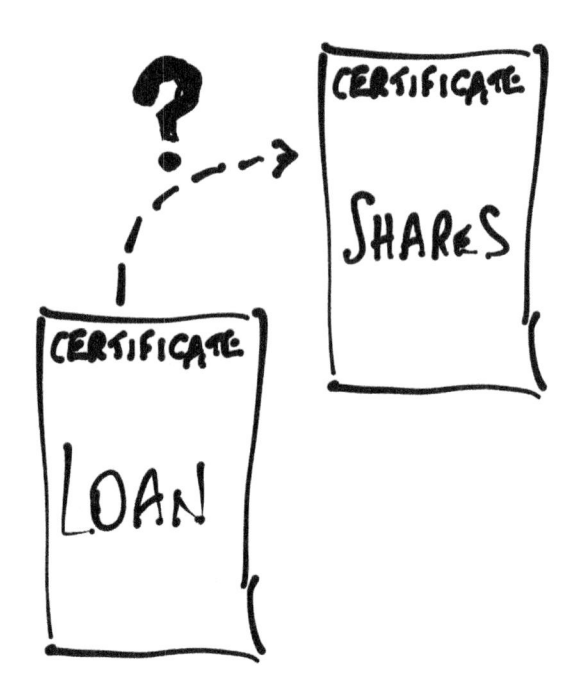

Convertible loans are only for the more sophisticated, experienced, borrower. I will try to explain what they are, when they are possibly attractive to use and some of the common misconceptions about them.

We used a Convertible Loan at one point, so it is probably easier if I use that as a real-life example.

The Convertible Loan is a form of secondary debt, so the lender only gets their money repaid after the primary lenders have been repaid. This means it is inherently riskier for the lender; so, they charge higher interest rates. Normally there are no bank covenants associated with secondary debt: it is only the primary lenders who use bank covenants.

The Convertible Loan had a fixed term. Let's say seven years. To ensure the lender got a decent return on their loan they would not allow repayment for three years. That meant they had at least three years being paid interest at the high rate. At the end of the three years we had the right to repay the loan. This is where the 'convertible' element of the loan kicked in.

Let's imagine the loan was £10 million. We would offer to repay the £10 million. The lender would then have to decide whether they wanted to accept the cash, or take £10 million worth of our shares instead, at a pre-agreed price. The key question for both the lender and the borrower then is "what share price do you use"? If, for example, the shares are priced at £4 then you would need to issue 2.5 million new shares to pay off the debt. If the share price was £2 then you would need to issue 5 million shares. The share price you use dictates how much of the company will be owned by the lender in future.

So, why did we decide to use this complex form of lending and how do you go about deciding a share price that will be fair to both lender and borrower?

We wanted to buy another company. We wanted to ensure our main bank covenant - the EBITDA:Net Debt Leverage Ratio was well below our limit, so that we had no chance of breaching it. We therefore had several choices:

1. Do we extend the size of our existing Revolving Credit Facility and reset the bank covenants? This would incur administration fees of about 1.5% of the loan amount

2. Do we issue new equity? If we issued new shares, what would be the price people would pay and how much of the company would the new owners' control i.e. what was the dilution?

3. Do we try to combine 1 and 2 and go for a Convertible Loan?

We rejected option 1 because it gave us access to more money, at the cost of an administration fee, but it pushed our Leverage ratio higher than we were comfortable with. Put simply, we would be too close to our bank covenants. After a successful decade, we didn't want to ever risk someone else taking control of our business.

The problem with option 2 was that we strongly believed that our share price was too cheap, and we would be selling shares below what we thought they were worth. Shareholders and directors of a publicly listed company like ours, almost always think their shares are worth more than they currently are. I will come back later to how you try to value shares fairly and take some of the emotion out of this decision.

We therefore decided that option 3 - using a Convertible Loan would be the best way forward. Our cashflow forecasts showed that we were very likely to be able to pay off the loan in three years, so there was a limit on how long we would have to pay the higher interest rates. We then reached an agreement with the lender that the share price that we would use to convert our loan into new shares would be 20% higher than today's share price. This reduced the number of new shares we would have to issue to pay off the loan considerably.

How did we persuade the lender to agree to convert their loan into shares at a share price that was 20% higher than today?

There were two parts to our strategy. The first involved trying to ascertain whether our current share price was fair or whether we were under-valued? The second part involved showing the estimated impact of the acquisition on the share price.

We discussed with the lender, the detail of our business plan and the impact of the proposed acquisition. We showed them the target share price once the deal had gone through. We then agreed to sell them shares at just below that price. So, if the acquisition was likely to increase our share price by 30% then we agreed to convert their shares at 20% higher than now ie we agreed to share some of the upside in the deal.

The second aspect of our proposal was to give them further confidence that our share price was likely to rise as it was currently undervalued. This involved creating a peer group of similar companies and demonstrating that we appeared to be cheaper than them for no apparently obvious reason. This was backed up by a series of research reports from technology analysts that calculated the target share price of our company. All of these analyses showed that we were undervalued, and our share price was likely to rise.

MY MESSAGE IS SIMPLE

Convertible loans are for sophisticated borrowers. They sometimes get a bad name because the interest rates are higher than normal and therefore people assume that you could not borrow money at normal, more attractive interest rates. They therefore assume there is something wrong with the company.

When people sat down and listened to the detailed logic of how we had found a way of issuing shares, at a much higher price than the current one, they tended to support the deal. Our problem was that many do not want to listen to the detail of a convertible loan.

As I said - this is one for the experienced borrowers only.

IS THIS THE REAL REASON, WHY THOMAS COOK FAILED?

I want to take a look at the collapse of Thomas Cook, the UK's 3rd largest travel agent and see if any of the lessons we have discussed apply?

Thomas Cook, founded in Market Harborough in 1841 by businessman Thomas Cook, was the world's first travel agent. Some 178 years later, it had grown to a huge global travel group, with annual sales of £9 billion, 19 million customers a year and 22,000 staff operating in 16 countries. [32]

---

[32] BBC, 2019. *Thomas Cook: What went wrong at the holiday firm?* [online]. Available at: < https://www.bbc.co.uk/news/business-46452374> [Accessed on 23 September 2019]

How does a business with £9billion sales per annum and 19 million customers go bankrupt?

The simple answer is that it could not repay its' bank loans.

Thomas Cook did not own its' own planes or hotels, so the loans were cashflow lending. At its peak in 2011, the total debt was £2 billion, when the pension deficit was included. In 2013 they raised £425 million from shareholders to reduce their debt burden. When it went bust in 2019 the debt was back to £1.6 billion.

In previous sections we have talked about the need for consistent cashflow and predictable forecasting when you are borrowing using cashflow. It is difficult to see how Thomas Cook met these criteria.

There are several factors that make financial predictions difficult with travel agents, many of which are outside their control: the weather, politics (in this case Brexit causing people to delay holidays or take them in the UK) and social changes such as the move to self-booked holidays and the rise of companies like AirBnB. If people delay booking their holidays, then they often get discounts for late bookings and the profits of companies like Thomas Cook are impacted as margins fall. It is even worse than that. If customers book holidays in advance, then they have to pay a deposit whereas you do not for late-booked holidays. That meant that Thomas Cook received less cash, later.

This meant that there was a huge difference between the cashflow of Thomas Cook in the first and second half of each year. In May 2019, Proactive reported that "Weaker trading resulted in free cash outflows of £839 million, compared to £718 million a year ago. Group net debt at the end of the period was £1.2 billion, up from £886 million last year. The company has secured a £300 million bank facility to provide additional liquidity for the winter 2019/20 season, subject to the sale of its airline business.[33]"

If you run a business that has big differences in cashflow for the first and second half of the year then you must be ready for the worst period, not the best. Given that first half bookings (and advance payments) are often driven by the weather - if the weather in the UK is very good then less feel the need to 'getaway' - cashflows were difficult to predict.

It would be easy to say that the world changed and the days of the package-

---

[33] Proactive, 2019. *Thomas Cook shares tumble as it posts wider first-half loss and warns of weaker second-half.* [online]. Available at: <https://www.proactiveinvestors.co.uk/companies/news/220390/thomas-cook-shares-tumble-as-it-posts-wider-first-half-loss-and-warns-of-weaker-second-half-220390.html> [Accessed on 16 May 2019]

holiday from companies like Thomas Cook were over, but this is not true. I think the problem was old-fashioned competition: newer companies who took their market share.

Travel Weekly reported that contrary to popular belief, Office for National Statistics figures showed that the number of overseas package holidays grew by 19% between 2013 and 2018. Between February 2015 and April 2019, the number of Thomas Cook passengers registered with ATOL (the travel insurance agency) fell by 36.7% whereas Tui passengers increased by 22.3% and the smaller company Jet2holidays grew by 216.7%.[34]

MY MESSAGE IS SIMPLE

A business with hugely cyclical cashflows is not well suited to high levels of debt as cashflows are difficult to predict. Often the 'gap' between a business plan supplied to a bank and the point at which you start to hit bank covenants is about 15%. Put another way: if you cannot predict accurate cashflows to within 15% then you should borrow only small amounts of money. Thomas Cook did the opposite - they borrowed huge amounts of money.

In an interview with the Sunday Times on 29th September 2019, Thomas Cook Chief Executive Peter Fankhauser said, "It's hard to change when you have a debt burden that high. We spent £1.2 billion in interest payments and debt refinancing since 2012. Imagine if I could have invested even half of that in IT, in the remaining shops, in the new hotels and other innovations."

There are two reasons a business can go bust. If the Company makes an Operating Loss, then the business does not deserve to survive. If a business makes sensible operating profits, but it has borrowed so much money that it cannot pay its' interest and loan repayments then you need to ask who decided to borrow so much money (when they could not afford it)?

---

[34] Travel Weekly, 2019. *Analysis: what brought down Thomas Cook?* [online]. Available at: <http://www.travelweekly.co.uk/articles/346047/analysis-what-brought-down-thomas-cook> [Accessed on 11th October 2019]

CHAPTER TEN
Pros and Cons of Floating on AIM

WHY WE REALLY FLOATED ON AIM

The part of the London Stock Exchange dedicated to smaller businesses is the Alternative Investment Market: known universally as AIM. Since its inception in 2005 and November 2019 there have been 3,867 companies floated on AIM and yet at the end of November 2019, only 872 remained.[35] This shows you how many small companies either fail, or change their mind and go private again; sometimes as a result of a take-over; often by private equity funds. In 2006, 462 companies floated on AIM and raised £15.67 billion. It seemed that AIM was the perfect answer to raising money for smaller businesses and the UK was once again leading the way. 2006 ended with a then record number of

---

[35] London Stock Exchange, 2019. *Aim statistics-november-2019,* [pdf] Available at: <https://www.londonstockexchange.com/statistics/markets/aim/aim.htm> [Accessed 29 December 2019]

1,634 companies listed on AIM. The number of companies increased slightly in 2007 to 1,694 but the companies floated were bigger and a new record amount of funds were raised - £16.183 billion. Between 2005 and November 2019 companies floating on AIM have collectively raised a staggering £115.188 billion. And yet one of the most common questions I am asked is whether I think in hindsight we were right to float on AIM and whether I would do it again? Why are people asking that? In 2008 the financial crash arrived and the picture on AIM changed quite dramatically. Between 2009 and 2019 the funds raised each year have ranged from £3.1 billion to £6.9 billion - a long way from the dizzy peaks of 2006 and 2007. In 2019 only 21 companies floated on AIM. There are now so many other ways of raising money that the perceived hassle of being a listed company has put many off.

So, what do I say when I am frequently asked about floating on AIM? It worked for us because we understood the problem we were trying to solve. Whenever you float on AIM the City wants you to sell some shares to raise money; often to fund an acquisition and grow quickly. So, we did that. We raised over £8 million and did an acquisition. Whilst this completely fitted in with our business plan it wasn't the driving force for floating and I felt sad that the City didn't seem to want to hear the real story ... We started AdEPT by about 12 of us putting in some money to raise £3.25 million in total. Our original idea was to buy several Telecoms companies and make them more profitable by merging them together. After three years we planned to sell the business and hopefully make some money. At the end of three years, the major shareholders who knew the business best, did not want to sell. As we learned more and more about our sector, we could see that the opportunity was bigger than we initially thought. However, we had accidentally trapped our friends. What do I mean by that?

Being a minority shareholder of a private company that does not pay dividends can be a terrible situation. You get no income, but you also have no say in when the business will be sold and therefore when you can get your money back. By floating on the London Stock Exchange, we created a situation whereby our initial shareholders could sell their shares whenever they wished. It was an honourable solution to a problem we had accidentally created.

MY MESSAGE IS SIMPLE

The first thing you need to do is to decide: what problem you are trying to solve? Then you need to examine the options you have for solving that problem. If you are trying to raise money, then there are a lot more options now than there were in 2006. Floating on AIM is simply one option and like all options it has its Pro's and Con's.

RUNNING PUBLIC AND PRIVATE COMPANIES

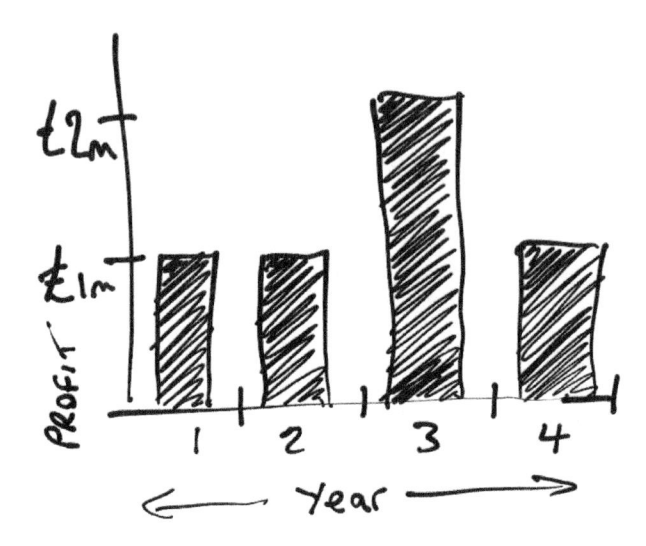

I have run both public and private companies and am often asked what the main difference is? Most people expect me to respond by talking about corporate governance and the various rules and regulations that you don't have when you are a private company. I never do. Instead I tell this story ...

Imagine that you and I ran a company that made £1 million profit in year 1 and £1 million profit again in year 2. In year 3 profit doubled to £2 million. In year 4 profit fell back to £1 million.

If this company was private then we would probably be in the pub drinking lager, remembering a record year, last year. "Absolutely fantastic last year - we made £2 million. We are back to normal now, making £1 million profit a year, but we'll never forget that great year".

If this was a public company, then the Chief Executive would probably be fired, for profits halving.

When you are running a public company, investors want to see that profits are predictable and sustainable. If profits drop, then your share price can fall heavily. If the profit drop is permanent, then the shares will fall to reflect this. If the profit drop is temporary, it is quite possible that no-one will believe it is temporary, until the results start to stabilise again. Unfortunately, that takes time; often at least two years.

This means that you sometimes become more risk averse when you run a public company. Let's look at an example.

If you hire several extra salespeople in an attempt to grow revenue, it can take time before you find out whether the new sales team are any good. Your profits will fall when you have the costs of the extra sales team, but they haven't sold anything (or much) yet. Let's assume, as often happens, that the new sales team did not work, and you then get rid of them.

If the company you are running is private, then no-one can see that your profits fell and then came back up again, when the sales team were let go. If you are running a public company, then this costly failure will be very visible for all to see.

MY MESSAGE IS SIMPLE

It is much easier to try things in a private company as you can have failures, and no-one can see what is happening.

Trying things that may not work is a lot less easy with a public company as you are 'living in a goldfish bowl' and everything you do can be seen by all who wish to look. In a public company you cannot hide your failures.

Having said that - there is a big difference between running, say, a small family owned private company and a larger private company owned by private equity. A private equity owner will be trying to improve and then sell the business in a three to five year timescale. They will probably be just as impatient as public company owners.

CHAPTER ELEVEN
Running A Board

WHY NOTHING SHOULD BE DECIDED BY ONE-MAN-ONE-VOTE

People often describe a democracy as 'one man one vote'. Some business owners seem to think that in business it means that they are the only man that has a vote. I think completely the opposite. You should never decide anything in business by a majority vote.

I know that it makes great drama when you are watching a film or TV programme when you see a Board gradually announcing their votes and there is tension trying to work out which side is going to win. But in real life the last thing you want, is a company that has two different factions, proposing different ways forward. Whoever loses a vote will always feel aggrieved.

Many bosses say to me that as the boss it is their prerogative to decide the way forward. I think that is dangerous. In nearly 30 years of being the boss I never decided anything by a split vote.

I regarded my voice as being equal to everyone else's. If I could not persuade people that my arguments were worth supporting, then either I was wrong, or I hadn't thought through how to explain my ideas effectively.

If you spot someone in the room, that does not appear to be comfortable with what is being proposed, then ask what their reservations are? If they can clearly explain their reservations, then you should listen to them carefully and work out how you are going to counter these arguments. If the person cannot explain why they feel uncomfortable then it is more likely that they simply do not understand what is being proposed and why?

MY MESSAGE IS SIMPLE

Do not underestimate the power of having a senior team that agree on a way forward. Everyone will pull hard in the same direction as they feel that they were part of the decision.

Conversely do not underestimate how difficult life can be when some senior managers do not agree with what the team is doing.

INSIDE AND OUTSIDE OF THE MEETING

I'm going to explain how much work and preparation I used to put into Board meetings, but to be honest, the same principles should apply to any meeting that is discussing something important.

We used to issue any slides or papers for the meeting at least 48 hours prior to the meeting, so that people had time to read them. I never allowed the person preparing the slides to send them out without me reviewing them first. This isn't paranoia; it is simply an understanding that your view is often shaped by what you read, and you need to ensure that issues are explained in the way that you want. If you are going to recommend something, ensure that the slides cover the logic and reasoning as to why this is the best way forward?

As Board meetings cover many subjects on one agenda it is inevitable that some items will be straightforward and quite routine. Normally only one or two items are likely to cause a more detailed debate. These are the ones that I used to socialise before the meeting. I would discuss the key items with each Board member individually by phone (if possible) a few days before to understand everyone's views.

I deliberately held the Board meetings at 10am, so that I could meet key influencers for breakfast before the meeting started. Many key decisions were agreed in advance at these breakfasts.

After the Board meeting we would all carry on to an informal lunch. This was a chance for everyone to have a chat outside of the formality of a Board meeting. It ensured that we had a forum where we could oscillate between work matters and important social issues such as football results.

MY MESSAGE IS SIMPLE

If it sounds like this is hugely formal, then you are missing the point. We used to eat together, drink together and laugh together. If you risk Board meetings or other important meetings being formal events where people just turn up and then leave immediately then you will find it hard to build a close-knit senior team.

Raising a potentially controversial issue without knowing in advance what everyone's view is can be very risky.

SHAREHOLDERS - AGREE OR ARGUE?

When you run any company, public or private, it can get complicated if you have major shareholders. One of the things that I learned quite early, much to my dismay, is that major shareholders do not necessarily agree with each other.

This means that it is almost impossible to please all of the people all of the time.

None of us like surprises. If you are thinking of doing anything major like raising money (from a bank or a share issue), or hiring a bigger salesforce, investing in a major capital expenditure project or doing an acquisition, then you must talk to your major shareholders before you do it. Even if you think they are likely to agree with your proposed plan of action few will thank you for telling them after the event.

It also gives the shareholder (or part-owner) a chance to object if they do not like the idea. It is important that you understand the reasons why? Listen carefully to their logic as major shareholders often have experience of working with other companies.

Try to understand whether their objection is something to do with the business and therefore would affect all other shareholders, or whether it is something specific to them? Let me give an example. Investment decisions are often impacted by tax regulations and these vary by country. What is good for UK investors can sometimes not work for an investor based in a different country with a different tax regime.

If the objections are something that could affect all shareholders, then go away and think about what they have said. It can be useful to talk to another shareholder to see if they have the same concerns and if not, why not?

It is also important that you are open with major shareholders and explain that other shareholders do not agree with them and the reasons why the other shareholders like the idea. A shareholder that is objecting to something needs to see that you, as the leader of the business, cannot please everyone.

MY MESSAGE IS SIMPLE

If you have major shareholders, it is very different to being sole owner of a business. There is bound to come a time when you will need their help or agreement; so, cultivate the relationship. If in doubt about what to do, then follow the simple maxim - treat your major shareholders the way you would like to be treated yourself.

If you are running a public company, then it gets a bit more complicated. There are very clear laws on insider information and what you can and cannot do. If in doubt always take advice about what you can and cannot say to people and when.

HOW TO USE A CHAIRMAN OR BOSS?

Many smaller businesses are run by the owner and do not have a Chairman. Many are successful, so it would be ridiculous to say that you can only succeed if you have a Chairman. Many see it as simply an extra, unnecessary cost. I disagree.

I am going to take a look at how in my experience an effective Chairman and Chief Executive works together and how there is a clear benefit to having a Chairman. Let's start by looking at what a Chairman does - and then I'll explain why I think none of the official definitions capture the essence of a good Chairman.

The UK Financial Reporting Council describes a Chairman like this ...

The **chairman** is responsible for leadership of the board and ensuring its effectiveness on all aspects of its role. Supporting Principle. The **chairman** is responsible for setting the board's agenda and ensuring that adequate time is available for discussion of all agenda items, in particular strategic issues.[36]

The (UK) Institute of Directors goes into more detail about what a Chairman should do …

The chairman's primary role is to ensure that the board is effective in its task of setting and implementing the company's direction and strategy.

The main features of the role of chairman are as follows:

- As well as being chairman of the board, he/she is expected to act as the company's leading representative which will involve the presentation of the company's aims and policies to the outside world.

- To take the chair at general meetings and board meetings. With regard to the latter this will involve: the determination of the order of the agenda; ensuring that the board receives accurate, timely and clear information; keeping track of the contribution of individual directors and ensuring that they are all involved in discussions and decision-making. At all meetings the chairman should direct discussions towards the emergence of a consensus view and sum up discussions so that everyone understands what has been agreed.

- To take a leading role in determining the composition and structure of the board. This will involve regular reviews of the overall size of the board, the balance between executive and non-executive directors and the balance of age, experience and personality of the directors.

- To ensure effective communication with shareholders and, where appropriate, the stakeholders.[37]

I don't disagree with these definitions, but I would never hire a Chairman and regard it as value-for-money if that is all they did. I don't want a Chairman to simply tick a box on a Corporate Governance Checklist. I want them to help make the business better.

---

[36] Financial Reporting Council, 2012. *The UK Corporate Governance Code.* [pdf]. Available at: <https://www.frc.org.uk/getattachment/e322c20a-1181-4ac8-a3d3-1fcfbcea7914/UK-Corporate-Governance-Code-(September-2012).pdf.> [Accessed on 2 January 2020]

[37] Institute of Directors (UK), 2018, *The Role of the Chairman.* [online] Available at: <https://www.iod.com/news/news/articles/The-role-of-the-chairman> [Accessed on 2 January 2020]

I have been looking back at what made Roger Wilson, my Chairman for 16 years at AdEPT, and I such an effective team. You will decide whether our mode of working works for you.

The safest choice of Chairman is someone you have worked with before. Roger and I had worked together twice before; that may not be possible for you. The second key point was that he was a shareholder. Our interests were completely aligned. I am a big fan of non-executive directors being shareholders as the only debates are about 'the best way to make money for all of us.' The third reason it worked so well was that he had a huge amount of experience in running businesses. He had been CEO and understood the pressures. More importantly he had huge experience in our sector. That meant that he could contribute knowledgeably to our debates. The fourth reason was that he was a great listener and questioner.

Roger became my mentor rather than a distant Chairman. I would ring him regularly and explain the problems I had found. I was completely open with him. Too many CEO's try to protect things from the Chairman given that the Chairman's ultimate sanction is to sack them and get another CEO. I believe in the opposite - two brains are always better than one and it helps significantly if the CEO and Chairman agree on most major issues. You do not want constant disagreements around a board table.

Now that I am Chairman, I find myself using the techniques he used on me for years.

The Chairman would ask me to explain the problem and then outline the various options we had, the pros and cons of each and why I had selected a particular way forward. It is amazing how trying to explain your logic out loud to someone else helps. If my explanation wasn't clear he would ask more probing questions. If I suddenly 'dried up' and couldn't clearly and simply explain why I didn't like an option, he would gently suggest that we should look at it in a bit more detail.

I think he was trying to avoid me relying on 'gut feel' decisions. There will be occasions when your 'gut feel' is right but if you use it regularly then you are just lazy and have not thought through the detail.

In particular you need to consider the consequences of your proposed actions. The law of unintended consequences is huge, but to be fair, most of the horrible consequences that sometimes happen, where predictable if you thought about the issue in detail.

MY MESSAGE IS SIMPLE

Being the boss can be lonely and having someone else to bounce ideas off is hugely valuable. The simple act of trying to explain your reasoning to someone else often finds flaws in your thought process.

Roger and I worked together as Chairman and CEO when we were a private business as well as later on as a public company. If you still think a Chairman is merely good for public companies then you have missed the point of my story.

CHAPTER TWELVE
Keeping Going

THE PERSONALISED HAT TRICK

We must have thousands, if not millions, of conversations in our lives. It is amazing that one or two conversations are remembered forever, and the rest are completely forgotten.

When I was in my early 40's I had a chat with a very successful businessman who was about 10 years older than me. I wanted to understand how he had kept his enthusiasm going, for so long? He still bubbled with enthusiasm when he talked about his company. His answer was not what I expected and that is possibly why I have remembered it and told this story so often.

He said, "When I was younger, I wanted to be captain of the England football team and score a hat-trick at Wembley. As I am now in my fifties, I've had to accept that it will never happen."

"Instead I have changed my definition of a hat-trick. Every year I pick three things I want to achieve, and I feel just as good, if I manage to get all three done".

I asked him what 'this years' hat-trick was?

He said, "I love helping the new sales team. They are all quite young. If we can win three contracts, valued at least £1 million each, then I'll be really happy".

It was July so I asked him how the 'hat-trick' was going? He laughed and said, "Scored two, five months to go".

MY MESSAGE IS SIMPLE

It is up to you to find your own version of the hat-trick; something that drives you on. It will be different for everyone. If you just drift along aimlessly then you will eventually run out of steam.

SOMETHING ONLY FOR YOU

It sounds glamorous being the boss, but the reality is that it can be lonely and when things are not going well, it can be a constant hard slog. The most successful people are the ones who do not give in and seem to find an inner strength from somewhere that keeps them going.

My recommendation is that you find something that means a lot to you, but not necessarily to anyone else. Something that drives you on and persuades you not to quit. I am happy to share with you the one that I used, but I'm not sure it is the right one for other people. I think you need to pick something personal.

Mine started as an accident. It dawned on me that every year since I had been made a Managing Director, or later CEO, EBITDA had risen every year. If you are not an accountant just think of EBITDA as a measure of profitability that is closest to estimating the cashflow of the firm. In a sense it doesn't really matter what it was. I was simply trying to beat last year - every year.

At first, I wanted to keep the record of rising EBITDA running for five years. Once I had reached five years, I decided to try for ten successive years - a decade of unbroken growth sounded great. When I changed companies, my aim was simply to beat whatever happened the previous year.

The longer it went on, the more obsessed I became, that this year would not be the end of the unbroken run of rising EBITDA. When I finally stood down as a CEO, I had the honour of announcing 29 consecutive years of rising EBITDA. I had never gone backwards.

It didn't matter that some years were well ahead of the year before and others had just scraped ahead. In some senses, the years when we only just beat the year before, were the most satisfying. I decided to tell my senior team about the record of rising EBITDA, although I only mentioned the years at that particular company. At my final company, AdEPT, we had 16 consecutive years of rising EBITDA and the senior team became as focused as I was at not losing the record. When we had really tough years, it gave us something to rally around that meant nothing to anyone else. The 'team' learned never to give in.

MY MESSAGE IS SIMPLE

There are going to be some down days and you need to work out what will keep you going. Do not expect your team to perk up the boss when they are having a bad day. That is your job. Giving in is easy. Keeping going is what will make you special.

No matter how stressed you are do not take it out on your team. Give them a reason to join you in never giving in. Winning when it is easy feels good, but it will never feel as special as when you win against all the odds. It is these victories and war stories that will bond people together.

RECESSIONS - WHAT TYPICALLY HAPPENS

William Keegan, the long-time economics Editor of The Observer looked back over the fifty years he was an economics journalist, in his book, 'Nine Crises'.[38] He identified nine periods of economic uncertainty over the fifty years to 2019. I decided to look at my twenty-nine years as a Managing Director/CEO and realised that I had managed through fourteen years of economic uncertainty.

If I had allowed economic uncertainty to become an excuse for falling profits, then roughly half of my twenty-nine years of rising profitability would have gone.

---

[38] William Keegan, 2019. *Nine Crises - Fifty Years of covering the British Economy from devaluation to Brexit.* 1st Ed. Biteback Publishing

You must never allow economic uncertainty to become an excuse as to why your business cannot grow its' profitability. Instead you should seek to understand the characteristics of what is happening. Whilst there are some unique factors in every period of economic uncertainty there are also many things that regularly happen and are highly predictable.

Let me tell you a story about TV and chocolate.

As soon as times look like they are getting harder, many families start to cut back on discretionary spend. One of the first things to go is normally the Friday or Saturday night visit to a family restaurant for a pizza or a burger. The £100-150 it used to cost is a relatively easy saving. Instead families tend to download the latest blockbuster film and get a big bar of chocolate. The young kids are probably happier being cuddled on the sofa, rather than bored, watching mum and dad drink wine.

You might think that I am being over-simplistic, but I am not. Just look at your own friends with young families.

Let's look at what else always happens. If you are a business contemplating a costly investment in new capital equipment - let's say a computer server upgrade, or a new fleet of wagons - then it is very likely you will delay the decision until your economic prospects are clearer.

MY MESSAGE IS SIMPLE

In a time of economic uncertainty, the first things that get cancelled are one-off 'nice-to-haves' that can wait if necessary. That is why I tried to ensure that every business I ran had at least 75% of its' sales revenue from recurring products or services - as an example - subscription revenues, monthly rentals, support contracts etc. The companies that suffered much greater swings in profitability were the ones that relied almost entirely on sales of one-off equipment or projects.

You must never base your business on what happens in the 'good times'. Every few years the economy will stumble again, and you need to be able to cope.

BUSINESS IS A PROBLEM-SOLVING EXERCISE

Some of the best businesspeople are the ones who can be successful in several different industries. They are the true serial entrepreneurs. I had the privilege of working with Alex, a gentleman who had been successful in industries as diverse as airlines, jewelry, recruitment, concrete, trucking and others I cannot remember as the list is so long.

When you meet someone like this you must listen closely to what they say and watch what they do.

He was a master at doing the right thing for staff. He recognised that happy, well-motivated, staff are the key. He would send old-fashioned thank you notes, flowers, bottles of wine etc to employees; from the receptionist to the directors and everyone in-between.

He used to say, "Business is a problem-solving exercise". "If I ask you what your problems are, and you say that you haven't got any then that simply shows that you do not know what is going on".

If you told him what your problems were and what you were doing to tackle them, he would rate you highly. He often offered alternative solutions for you to mull over. He never told you what to do; he simply invited you to think in a different way.

MY MESSAGE IS SIMPLE

In your career you only meet a few people like this, and you should cherish their advice and learn as much as you can from them. The best businesspeople are the ones that admit they have problems, show that they understand what their problems are and have evaluated the options they have, before deciding what to do?

The poorer managers are the ones who think that admitting to having problems is a sign of weakness.

CHAPTER THIRTEEN
All Good Things Come to An End

PLANNING THE HANDOVER

Many businesses are run by a founder that has been in charge for many years. When it comes time for the founder to finally stand down, the change is inevitably scary, for all affected.

I was the founder and Chief Executive of AdEPT for 16 years. How did I go about handing over to a new Chief Executive in a way that guaranteed consistency and continuity for the business and did not spook any of the key investors? The last thing we wanted was a big drop in the share price.

There are lots of ways doing handovers. Our plan worked well, so I thought I would share it with you, and you can decide whether it would work for you?

Right from the start I had a 12-month notice period in my contract. It gave me and my family protection, but it was primarily to assure investors, that I would never leave suddenly without warning. In December 2016, two years before I stood down, I wrote to the Board formally and told them that I was thinking of serving 12-months' notice in one years' time. This gave all of us a year to get used to the idea. It also allowed me to be certain before I finally gave 12-months' notice and in effect planned a move into part-time retirement.

During 2017 we decided that the best way to guarantee consistency and continuity was if I moved up to be two days a week Chairman. I promised to serve at least two years in this part-time capacity, and we agreed a salary package. This gave me the confidence to formally resign with 12-months' notice in December 2017.

The Board agreed that we did not have anybody internally with enough experience, to become the new Chief Executive, so we hired a firm of headhunters. I met them along with the non-executive directors. I explained to the headhunters what I thought we needed from a new CEO and the non-executive directors added their take on the situation.

The first thing that we agreed was that my replacement should have different skills to me; but should share the same values about how you treat people and run a business. After several acquisitions we had changed from being a Telecoms company into primarily an IT managed service business. We therefore needed someone with experience of IT rather than Telecoms. We also wanted someone with a sales and marketing background as my experience was primarily finance, operations and acquisitions.

I spoke individually to each of the large investors and explained the logic of what we were thinking of doing and the way in which we were approaching it. They all bought into the process and that made it much easier.

We hired Phil Race and appointed him in a new role: Group Managing Director. As this was not initially a PLC Board director role, we did not need to announce this to the Stock Exchange. Phil and I then went to every meeting together for four months. At the end of the meeting we would discuss what he thought of the issues discussed in the previous meeting and just as important, his impression of the people who had taken part.

At the end of each month, Phil was brave enough to present to me (don't forget I was CEO for the previous sixteen years) his impressions of the 'strengths and weaknesses' of the organisation and what we needed to do in our next stage of development when he would be the leader.

In the early presentations I accepted most of his observations, but not all. As the months went by, we got closer and closer to the finally agreed plan. This way we knew that the business was not going to suddenly change course and the new Chairman (me) and CEO (Phil) would have little chance to disagree on anything in the first few months. The last thing we wanted was a new

Chairman and new CEO at loggerheads.

I am not a great fan of creating some elaborate handover plan. The danger is that you send the new boss into lots of visits and meetings without any guidance. They can easily pick up the wrong end of the stick. I lost count of the times I said something like, "If it looks strange, then accept we are not stupid people and why don't you ask the historical reason for it?"

We also decided that as two-day a week Chairman I would continue to attend the Monday morning meeting with the CEO and CFO, later joined by the COO as well. This guaranteed that both of us remained close to all major decisions. To further guarantee consistency we continued to use the standard agenda that had served us well for sixteen years.

I was also new to the role of Chairman; after being a Managing Director or Chief Executive for twenty-nine years. I therefore asked our Chairman, Roger Wilson, to remain as Deputy Chairman for another fifteen months (until the end of the financial year). I needed someone that I could turn to, to help me become a Chairman. I also needed someone who knew me well enough to ring me, without me asking, whenever he saw me potentially making a mistake.

MY MESSAGE IS SIMPLE

The longer you plan a changeover the better it will be. The more you involve the key stakeholders the better; as no-one likes surprises.

At the end of the day the ultimate success of a new CEO will be judged by the results they deliver. However, anything you can do to make their early months as easy as possible, must help.

IF IT WAS EASY, EVERYONE WOULD BE DOING IT

When the TV talent show programme the X Factor first started, like many, I enjoyed it. However, I quickly started to worry that X Factor and other reality TV programmes were convincing many young people that fame and fortune can be achieved in 15 minutes.

The reality is that there is only one X Factor winner in a country of around 60 million people. On a much bigger scale; on a planet that had 7.7 billion people in April 2019 there is only one Facebook. We must recognise that success like this happens to almost no-one.

A business book like this is not a recipe book. If you follow the lessons on every page, it is still no guarantee that your new business will succeed, or your business career will prosper. I hope you have learned some things from this book and if it has inspired you to pursue a career in business then that is wonderful. Every country needs successful businesses to create employment and improve the economic well-being of society. We need people employed and paying taxes or the Government has no money to spend on the services we all need.

I grew up with an 'old-fashioned work ethic,' but I think there is absolutely nothing old-fashioned about having a strong work ethic. If you look at the difference between those that succeed in business and those that do not, then it is rarely about academic qualifications. If it was purely about IQ and academic qualifications, then the richest people in the world would all be professors.

I think the biggest difference is that the outstanding businesspeople try incredibly hard and rarely give in when they have knock-backs. Remember the story about the number of failures that Richard Branson has had.

MY MESSAGE IS SIMPLE

If it was easy; everyone would be doing it.

ACKNOWLEDGEMENTS

This is the first time I have written a book and the experience has been amazing. I can't over-exaggerate how scary it is to hand your draft manuscript to someone you respect to have a read. You want them to make helpful comments, but inside you really want them to say that it is just great as it is.

Everyone who helped me was asked what they liked as well as what they didn't. First time authors need encouragement as well.

I gave the draft book initially to my long-time mentor Roger Wilson and Alex Birchall, a serially successful entrepreneur. Starting with some very experienced businesspeople was both daunting and ultimately very encouraging.

To get a wider range of views from people of all ages and experience, I asked if any of our 300+ employees would like to help. Over 40 people agreed to join my project and they jokingly became referred to as 'The Street-Smart MBA Proof-readers Club'. It is a very long list, so I won't name everyone: you all know who you are, and I can't thank you enough.

A journalist, who I don't even know, and never met, was given a copy and he gave me some hugely helpful pointers. Whoever you are: I am amazed by your generosity.

The detailed comments provided by Craig Wilson, one of the most senior CEO's in the UK IT industry were whatever the next level is beyond 'thought provoking'.

When the book was finally published, I was 59 3/4 years old. I hope this encourages everyone who has ever said, "One day I'll write a book," that you are never too old to start.

ABOUT THE AUTHOR

Ian Fishwick is married with two adult daughters. He lives in Kent, England.

COPYRIGHT

Copyright © 2020 Ian Fishwick

All rights reserved. No part of this book may be reproduced in any form or by any electronic or mechanical means, including information storage and retrieval systems, without written permission from the author, except in the case of a reviewer, who may quote brief passages embodied in critical articles or in a review. Trademarked names appear throughout this book. Rather than use a trademark symbol with every occurrence of a trademarked name, names are used in an editorial fashion, with no intention of infringement of the respective owner's trademark. The information in this book is distributed on an "as is" basis, without warranty. Although every precaution has been taken in the preparation of this work, neither the author nor the publisher shall have any liability to any person or entity with respect to any loss or damage caused or alleged to be caused directly or indirectly by the information contained in this book.

Printed in Great Britain
by Amazon